Using Primary Sources to Teach U.S. History
War to Constitution

Written by Rebecca Stark

The purchase of this book entitles the individual teacher to reproduce copies of the student pages for use in his or her classroom exclusively. The reproduction of any part of the work for an entire school or school system or for commercial use is prohibited.

ISBN 978-1-56644-570-2

© 2017 Barbara M. Peller, AKA Rebecca Stark
EDUCATIONAL BOOKS 'N' BINGO

Printed in the United States of America.

Table of Contents

INTRODUCTION 5

AMERICAN REVOLUTION BACKGROUND INFORMATION 6–7

Benjamin Franklin's "Join or Die" Cartoon 8–9
The Stamp Act and the Sons of Liberty 10–11
The Stamp Act: Protest and Repeal 12–15
The Boston Massacre...16–17
The Boston Tea Party...18–20
Patrick Henry 21–24
Thomas Paine 25–27
Declaration of Independence 28–31
Burgoyne's Surrender at Saratoga 32–35
Spies in the American Revolution 36–37
Valley Forge 38–40
Marquis de Lafayette 41–42
John Paul Jones 43–45
Paying for the War: Robert Morris 46–48
Paying for the War: Haym Salomon 49
Siege of Yorktown 50–54
Articles of Confederation 55–57
Treaty of Paris 58–61
Shays' Rebellion 62–65
The United States Constitution 66–69
The Federalist Papers 70–72
The United States Constitution: Signing the Document 73–74
George Washington's First Inauguration 75–77
The Bill of Rights 78–79

APPENDIX WITH TRANSCRIPTIONS AND LINKS TO IMAGES 81–94

ANSWER SECTION... 95–104

DOCUMENT ANALYSIS SHEETS 105–108

Using Primary Sources in the Classroom

Primary sources are original materials from the past. They comprise birth certificates, legal documents, speeches, letters, diary entries, ledgers, political cartoons, posters, advertisements, stamps, photographs, maps, newspaper articles, and other first-hand records. Primary sources help us to understand the period in which they were created and to gain insight into the people of that period.

The study of primary sources engages students in active learning and encourages higher-level thinking. Students are given opportunities to use their inferencing skills to interpret the documents and other items they analyze. They also use important application, analysis, and evaluation skills. By examining a variety of documents on the same topic, students develop an understanding that people interpret events from differing points of view.

Another benefit that can be derived from the study of primary sources is that students often rethink preconceived notions about people and events. They come to realize that their biases and prejudices may be based upon faulty information. By learning how people from the past felt, they often develop empathy for those people.

ABOUT THIS BOOK

Background material regarding the subject is provided. Following this information are Think About It activities, which present challenging activities to promote critical-thinking skills.

Complete transcripts of some of the larger documents are provided in the Appendix. The original spellings and grammatical errors are retained.

Comprehensive answers and additional background information are provided in the Answer Section.

Document Analysis Worksheets are provided for a few types of primary-source materials. These worksheets were designed and developed by the Education Staff, National Archives and Records Administration, Washington, DC 20408. You will find them at the end of this resource.

SUGGESTIONS

Vocabulary
Instruct students to make a list of unfamiliar vocabulary as they read. Ask them to use context clues to figure out the meanings of words they do not know and if they are not sure, to look up them up in a dictionary. Help students as needed with difficult spellings in the original documents.

Images
Have the students find color versions of some of the images online. Elicit from them how seeing them in color enhanced the experience.

**The use of primary sources in your classroom can bring
history to life for you and your students. Enjoy the journey!**

The American Revolution
Background Information

Also known as the United States War for Independence, the American Revolution was a conflict between the Thirteen Colonies and Great Britain. Tensions between the colonists and the colonial governments representing the British crown began about 1765 and grew steadily. In April 1775 the early skirmishes at Lexington and Concord marked the start of colonies' revolt against British rule. A few months later the war was in full swing.

The Patriots, or Revolutionaries, were determined to gain independence from Great Britain, and on June 14, 1775, the Second Continental Congress formed the Continental Army.

Benjamin Franklin's "Join or Die" Cartoon—Benjamin Franklin first published his "Join or Die" cartoon on May 9, 1754, in the *Pennsylvania Gazette,* a Philadelphia newspaper owned by him. His message was originally meant to unite the colonies on the side of Britain against the French and their Indian allies. It was later used to encourage the colonists to unite against Britain.

The Stamp Act and the Sons of Liberty—The Sons of Liberty was a secret society formed in 1765 with the purpose of protecting the colonists against unfair taxation without representation, especially the Stamp Act.

The Stamp Act: Protest and Repeal—This was the first internal tax levied directly on American colonists by the British government. It imposed a tax on newspapers and all other paper documents in the colonies. The colonists considered the act to be illegal.

The Boston Massacre—This incident took place on March 5, 1770, on King Street in the Massachusetts Bay Colony. A squad of British soldiers were being heckled with snowballs and taunts. In response, they shot and killed 5 colonists.

The Boston Tea Party—This incident was a political protest arranged by the Sons of Liberty in Boston, Massachusetts, on December 16, 1773, to protest the Tea Act. Dressed as Native Americans, the colonists dumped the tea in the river.

Patrick Henry—This Virginian attorney, planter, and statesman is best known for his "Give Me Liberty or Give Me Death" speech, which he delivered to the Second Virginia Convention, on March 23, 1775. In it he proposed the organization of a volunteer militia and expressed the opinion that war was inevitable.

Thomas Paine—Thomas Paine was a political activist best known for his pamphlet *Common Sense*. He encouraged the colonists to declare their independence from Great Britain.

Declaration of Independence—The Declaration of Independence was adopted on July 4, 1776, by the Second Continental Congress.

Battles of Saratoga—The Saratoga campaign gave a decisive victory to the Americans and marked a turning point in the war.

Spies in the American Revolution: Benedict Arnold—Benedict Arnold was a general in the American Continental Army who later defected to the British side and plotted the surrender of West Point.

Valley Forge—General Washington headquartered at Valley Forge from December 19, 1777, to June 18, 1778. The very harsh winter was very difficult. However, in the spring, Baron von Steuben helped transform the threadbare troops into a fighting force.

Marquis de Lafayette—Lafayette, a French aristocrat and military officer, fought on the side of the Continental Army in the American Revolutionary War. He spent the harsh winter at Valley Forge with General Washington and his men. He also helped by purchasing uniforms and muskets for them.

John Paul Jones—Jones was a naval commander in the American Revolution.

Paying for the War—Robert Morris, a Liverpool-born American merchant, is known as the "Financier of the American Revolution." Haym Salomon, a Polish-born Jewish immigrant, also played an important role in financing the war.

Siege of Yorktown—British troops led by General Cornwallis formally surrendered at Yorktown, Virginia, in 1781. This ended the last major campaign of the American Revolution.

Articles of Confederation—The Articles of Confederation, the first constitution of the United States, was adopted by the Continental Congress on November 15, 1777; however, the document was not adopted by all thirteen states until March 1, 1781.

Treaty of Paris of 1783—The Treaty of Paris of 1783 officially ended the American Revolutionary War and recognized America's independence from Great Britain. John Adams, Benjamin Franklin, John Jay, Thomas Jefferson, and Henry Laurens negotiated the treaty for the Americans.

Shays' Rebellion— This was the first major armed rebellion in the post-Revolutionary United States. In 1787, poor farmers from western Massachusetts, who were fighting against high taxes, followed Daniel Shays in an attempt to seize the arms stockpiled at the Springfield Armory.

The United States Constitution—The U.S. Constitution is the supreme law of the United States of America, It was signed by the delegates on September 17, 1787. On June 21, 1788, New Hampshire became the ninth state to ratify it. The Confederation Congress established March 4, 1789, as the date to begin operating a new government under the Constitution.

The Federalist Papers—The Federalist Papers was a collection of 85 articles and essays written by Alexander Hamilton, James Madison, and John Jay. The articles promoted ratification of the Constitution.

George Washington's First Inauguration—Washington was inaugurated as the first President of the United States on Thursday, April 30, 1789, on the balcony of Federal Hall in New York City, New York.

The Bill of Rights—The Bill of Rights are the first 10 amendments to the Constitution, written by James Madison in response to concerns about constitutional protection for individual liberties.

Benjamin Franklin
"Join or Die"

Background Information

Although he was born in Boston, Massachusetts, Benjamin Franklin spent most of his adult life in Philadelphia, Pennsylvania. He was a man of wide-ranging talents and knowledge. Even before he became active in the revolutionary movement, he had gained worldwide renown as an author, printer, publisher, scientist, inventor, and diplomat. In 1737 Franklin was appointed Postmaster of Pennsylvania and in 1775 he became the first Postmaster of the United States Post Office.

When the decision to declare independence was made in 1776, Benjamin Franklin collaborated with John Adams to advise Thomas Jefferson in his drafting of the Declaration of Independence. Franklin and Adams traveled to France and succeeded in obtaining an alliance with France. After the war ended, the two men also played an important role in negotiating the Treaty of Paris of 1783.

Portrait by Joseph Duplessis

Benjamin Franklin was a participant in the Constitutional Convention of 1787. Fifty-five delegates from twelve states attended; Rhode Island was the only state not to send any delegates. On September 17 of that year, 39 of them signed the document. At 81 years of age, Benjamin Franklin was the oldest. He had also been the oldest to sign the Declaration of Independence.

Although Benjamin Franklin played many important roles in the development of the new nation, it is as a printer and publisher that he had the most influence. In 1728 he became co-owner of a print shop in Philadelphia. The following year he also took over a Philadelphia newspaper, *The Pennsylvania Gazette*.

A few years later, Franklin published the first edition of *Poor Richard's Almanack*. After his description of his kite experiment in a later edition of this publication, interest in his scientific ideas and experiments spread, both in the colonies and in Europe.

Join or Die

On May 9, 1754, Benjamin Franklin published "Join or Die" in *The Pennsylvania Gazette*. The cartoon is said to be the first political cartoon in U.S. history. It accompanied Franklin's editorial, which was designed to encourage the colonists to fight the French and their Native American allies. The end goal was for British to gain and hold control over the land west of the Appalachian Mountains.

"Join or Die" acquired a different meaning when unrest brought about by the Stamp Act and other actions caused many colonists to protest British rule.

From *The Pennsylvania Gazette,* May 9, 1754

Think About It

1. This cartoon was used as a header in newspapers throughout the colonies with and without changes. Why was this possible?

2. What do the 8 abbreviations on the cartoon mean? Does the fact that there are only 8 surprise you? Research and analyze why there were only 8. Do you notice anything about their order?

3. During this period of time there was a superstition regarding snakes. Research and find out what it was and analyze how the myth might have affected the power of the cartoon.

4. Judge the use of political cartoons such as this one to persuade others to join a cause.

5. "Join or Die" has been called an example of an either/or fallacy. Explain why you agree or disagree with this evaluation.

The Stamp Act
Taxation without Representation

Background Information

When the Stamp Act was passed by the British Parliament in 1765, the colonists were already upset by the passage of the Sugar and Currency Acts of 1764. However, with this new act their unrest intensified.

The Stamp Act was a direct taxation on the colonists. It required all printed materials to carry a stamp. These stamps, which had to be purchased from a government agent, served as proof that the tax had been paid. Newspapers, books, posters, almanacs, dice, land deeds, and legal documents of all sorts were just some of the materials itemized along with the corresponding tax for each. Because the documents listed in the act included just about every imaginable use of a "skin or piece of vellum or parchment, or sheet or piece of paper, on which shall be ingrossed, written, or printed," all of the colonists were affected.

Protests mounted throughout the colonies, and in October 1765 delegates from nine colonies met in New York City. In their petition to the king, they affirmed their loyalty to the Crown, but also insisted that only the colonial representatives have the right to impose taxes on them. Nothing changed until March 1766, when Parliament repealed the Stamp Act. The people most responsible for that repeal were the Sons of Liberty.

Sons of Liberty

The Sons of Liberty was a secret society formed in reaction to the Stamp Act. Many believe that the organization was founded by Sam Adams, but that is not clear. The group's slogan was "No taxation without representation."

At first there were two main branches: one in Boston, which met under the Liberty Tree, and one in New York, which met under the Liberty Pole. Before long, there were Sons of Liberty groups in every colony.

Angry mobs prevented ships carrying the stamps to unload their cargoes. But the main goal of the protesters was to encourage excise collectors to resign, and they often resorted to violent means to achieve that goal. By the start of 1766, most stamp distributors had resigned, and Parliament had no choice but to repeal the despised act. On March 18 Parliament voted to repeal.

Portrait of Samuel Adams
by John Singleton Copley

The Stamp Act of 1765
Long Title and Request to Enact

Stamp Act of 1765

An act for granting and applying certain stamp duties, and other duties, in the British colonies and plantations in America, towards further defraying the expences of defending, protecting, and securing the same; and for amending such parts of the several acts of parliament relating to the trade and revenues of the said colonies and plantations, as direct the manner of determining and recovering the penalties and forfeitures therein mentioned.

WHEREAS by an act made in the last session of parliament, several duties were granted, continued, and appropriated, towards defraying the expences of defending, protecting, and securing, the British colonies and plantations in America: and whereas it is just and necessary, that provision be made for raising a further revenue within your Majesty's dominions in America, towards defraying the said expences: we, your Majesty's most dutiful and loyal subjects, the commons of Great Britain in parliament assembled, have therefore resolved to give and grant unto your Majesty the several rates and duties herein after mentioned; and do most humbly beseech your Majesty that it may be enacted, and be it enacted by the King's most excellent majesty, by and with the advice and consent of the lords spiritual and temporal, and commons, in this present parliament assembled, and by the authority of the same, That from and after the first day of November, one thousand seven hundred and sixty five, there shall be raised, levied, collected, and paid unto his Majesty, his heirs, and successors, throughout the colonies and plantations in America which now are, or hereafter may be, under the dominion of his Majesty, his heirs and successors,

Declaratory Act of 1766
An Act for the better securing the Dependency of His Majesty's Dominions in America upon the Crown and Parliament of Great Britain

Think About It

1. What did you learn about the reason for the Stamp Act from reading the long title?

2. To whom is Parliament requesting the enactment of this act?

3. When Parliament repealed the Stamp Act, it also issued the Declaratory Act. Research and find out the main purpose of this act. What do you think was the reaction of the colonists?

The Sons of Liberty
Protesting the Stamp Act

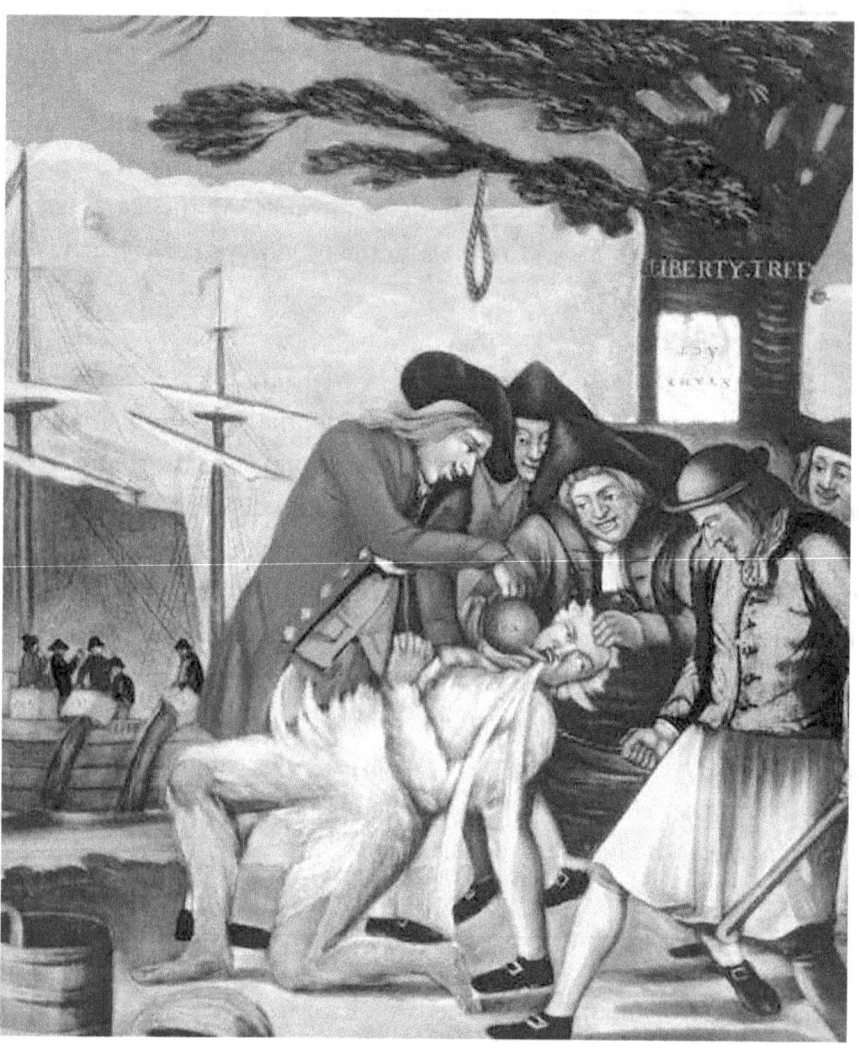

This is a British representation of the Bostonians' treatment of a British customs officer, John Malcom.

The BOSTONIANS Paying the EXCISE-MAN,
or _____ & _____
Source: Library of Congress.

THINK ABOUT IT
1. Fill in the blanks to complete the title of the engraving. The words describe how the Bostonian is "paying" the excise man.

2. Whom does the artist blame for this act? How do you know? What do you think is the artist's view of those to blame?

3. Protest stamps became common. People attached skull-and-bones stamps to documents to voice their disapproval. Many colonial newspapers used stamps, such as the one below at the right, to express their prediction of how the stamps would affect the future of journalism. Use details to explain their view of that effect.

12 *Using Primary Sources to Teach U.S. History: War to Constitution* © **Barbara M. Peller**

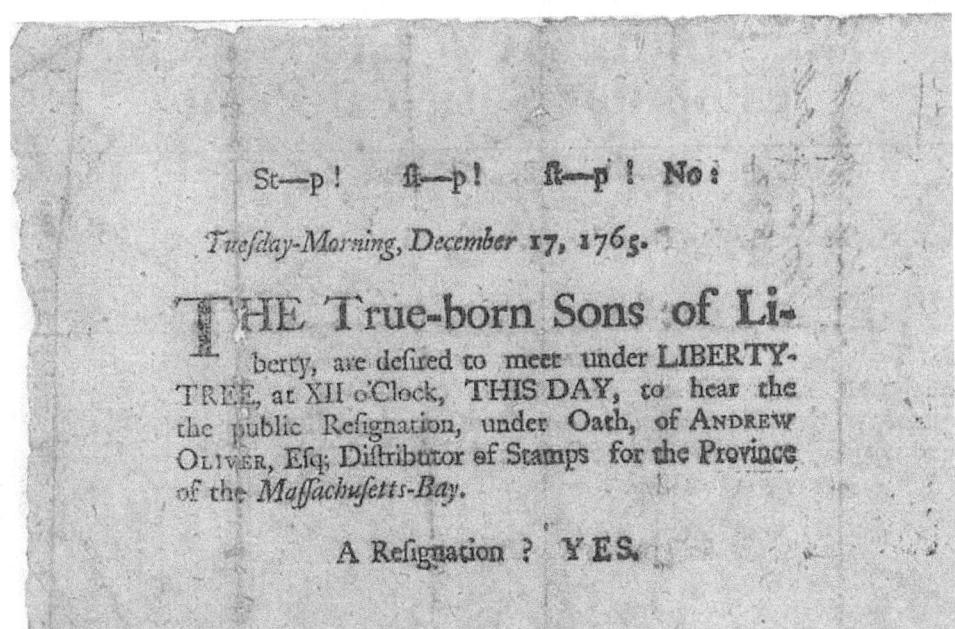

Author: Sons of Liberty

TRANSCRIPTION

St—p! St—p! St—p! No:

Tuesday-Morning, December 17, 1765 .

THE True-born Sons of Li-

berty, are desired to meet under LIBERTY-

TREE, at XII o'Clock, THIS DAY, to hear the

public Resignation, under Oath, of Andrew

Oliver, Esq; Distributor of Stamps for the Province

of the Massachusetts-Bay.

A Resignation ? YES.

4. The notice was printed as a broadside, or one-page hand-out. What did it announce?

5. According to the notice, when and where will the event take place?

6. Why did the Sons of Liberty choose this place for the event?

7. Why might they have felt it was necessary to call themselves the "True-born Sons of Liberty"?

8. What do you notice about the Colonial Era formation of the lower-case "s"? What editorial change would you make in the notice if you were the proofreader?

The Stamp Act: The Repeal
A Popular Satirical Print

Attributed to Benjamin Wilson (March 18, 1766) Prints and Photographs Division, Library of Congress

Transcription of the too-small-to-read text:

[Above the Vault] Within this Family Vault, Lie Interred, it is to be hoped never to rise again, The Star Chamber Court Ship Money Excise Money & all Imposts without Parliament. The Act de Haeritico Comburendo Hearth Mon Gener Warrants And which tended to alienate the Affections of Englishmen to their Country.

[Below the Visual] Over the Vault are placed two Skeleton Heads. Their elevation on Poles, and the dates of the two Rebellion Years, sufficiently shew what Party they espoused, and in what cause they suffered an ignominious Exit.

The reverend Mr. Anti-Sejanus (who under that signature hackney'd his pen in support of the Stamps) leads the procession as officiating Priest, with the burial service and funeral sermon in his hands.

Next follow two eminent Pillars of the Law, supporting two black flags, on which are delineated the Stamps with the White Rose and Thistle interwoved, an expressive design, supposed to have been originally contrived on the 10 of June. The significative motto Semper Eadem is preserved, but the Price of the Stamp is changed to three farthings, an important sum taken from the Budget. The numbers 122 and 71 declare the minority which fought under these Banners.

Next appears the honourable Mr. George Stamp, full of Grief and dispair, carrying his favourite Childs Coffin, Miss Americ Stamp, who was born in 1763 and died hard in 1766.

Immediately after, follows the chief Mourner Sejanus.

Then his Grace of Spital Fields, and Lord Gawkee.

After these Jemmy Twitcher, with a Catch, by way of funeral anthem, & by his side his friend and partner Mr. Falconer Donaldson of Halifax.

The rear is brought up by two right reverend Fathers of the Church.

These few mourners are separated from the joyful scene which appears on the River Thames, where three first rate ships are riding. VIZ. the Conway, Rockingham, and Grafton. Along the opposite Shore, stand open Warehouses, for the several goods of different manufacturing towns from which Cargoes are now shipping for America. Among these is a large Case containing the Statue of Mr. Pitt, which is heaving on board a Boat No. 250, there is another boat taking in goods nearer the first Rates, which is No. 105. These Numbers will ever be held in esteem by the true SONS of LIBERTY.

❀❀❀❀❀❀❀❀❀❀❀❀❀❀❀❀❀❀

Think About It

1. What is being portrayed? Does the cartoon show the bias of the creator?

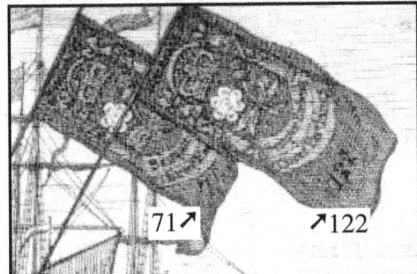

2. Who will lead the service?

3. The mourners following the leader are Solicitor General Wedderburn and Attorney General Norton. In your opinion, why are they referred to as "Two Pillars of the Law" in the text?

4. According to the text, "George Stamp" is holding the coffin. Who is George Stamp? Who (or what) is in the coffin?

5. The numbers 71 and 122 are on the black flags. What do the numbers represent?

6. What do the names of the ships in the background represent: "Conway," "Rockingham," and "Grafton"?

7. What purpose does the small dog in the foreground serve?

8. What was the purpose of the cartoon? Who was the intended audience?

© Barbara M. Peller

The Boston Massacre
Paul Revere's Print

Background Information

The Boston Massacre is the name given to the fatal shooting of five colonists by British soldiers. The event was the culmination of the unrest which began with the passage of early acts, such as the Sugar Act and the Stamp Act, and which grew with the Townshend Acts. Much of the protesting against them was centered in Boston.

When British troops were sent to Boston in October 1768 to enforce the collection of taxes, the colonists were outraged and unrest intensified. On the night of March 5, 1770, a group of colonists were taunting a squad of British soldiers. Members of the mob provoked the soldiers by throwing snowballs, sticks, and stones at them. The soldiers, who were there to keep order, instead lost control and opened fire on the men in the crowd, killing five of them. The first to fall was a black man named Crispus Attucks, a runaway slave who is now known as the first person killed in the American Revolution.

The Trials

A grand jury issued murder indictments against Captain Preston, who was in charge of the squad, and the eight soldiers in the squad. Four colonists accused of firing shots from a window in the Custom House were also indicted. The men were tried separately. It was difficult to find a lawyer to represent Captain Preston or the British soldiers, but finally, John Adams agreed to take on the task.

Captain Preston's trial revolved around one main question: Who gave the order to shoot by shouting, "Fire!" Fifteen witnesses testifying for the prosecution swore that Preston gave the order. When Adams cross-examined them, however, their testimony seemed contradictory. Also, witnesses for the defense testified that members of the crowd had provoked the soldiers. Captain Preston was acquitted on the basis of "reasonable doubt." It is thought that this was the first time that a judge used this phrase that has become such an important factor in our law.

The soldiers' trials became more complicated with the captain's acquittal. In their defense, John Adams said that their lives had been endangered and that they fired in self-defense. Six of the soldiers were acquitted on all counts, and two of them were convicted of the lesser charge of manslaughter.

The four colonists were acquitted.

The reputation of John Adams as a great lawyer spread throughout Massachusetts. In 1771 he was elected to the Massachusetts House of Legislature and years later he would become the second President of the United States.

While President, he looked back at his experience of defending Captain Preston and the soldiers:

> "The Part I took in Defence of Cptn. Preston and the Soldiers, procured me Anxiety, and **Obloquy** enough. It was, however, one of the most gallant, generous, manly and disinterested Actions of my whole Life, and one of the best Pieces of Service I ever rendered my Country. Judgment of Death against those Soldiers would have been as foul a Stain upon this Country as the Executions of the Quakers or Witches, anciently. As the Evidence was, the Verdict of the Jury was exactly right."

Paul Revere's print "The Bloody Massacre Perpetuated in King Street" was copied by him from a design by Henry Pelham. It first appeared on or about March 28, 1770, and soon became a great propaganda tool. Others, including Pelham, tried to sell similar prints, but Revere got his out so quickly that he had flooded the market.

Think About It

1. As John Adams, describe what went through your mind when deciding whether or not to take the case.

2. Analyze the print and explain the several inaccuracies.

3. The Customs House is seen behind the British soldiers. What change was made to the Customs House?

4. In your opinion, does the print support the guilt or innocence of Captain Preston? Explain.

5. Evaluate the name Boston Massacre to describe what happened on that day.

The Boston Tea Party
Protesting the Tea Act

Background Information

The Boston Tea Party was the name given to a political protest that took place on December 16, 1773, at Griffin's Wharf in Boston Harbor. Many factors led up to the unrest that culminated in this incident, but the thing most directly related to it was the Tea Act. When Parliament passed it on May 10, 1773, taxes on all goods except tea had already been repealed. This act did not add any new taxes; in fact, it made the price of tea less expensive for the colonists. However, the Tea Act permitted the British East India Company to sell their tea directly to the colonists at a lower price. The result was that it gave the British East India Company a monopoly on the sale of tea in the colonies.

It was not surprising that the act upset many tea merchants, including those who had become wealthy smuggling tea. On the night of December 16, 1773, three ships owned by Americans but carrying tea from the British East India Company were moored in Boston Harbor. They were the *Dartmouth,* the *Eleanor,* and the *Beaver.* Sam Adams, a leader in the Sons of Liberty, called a meeting at the Old South Church. Thousands attended. Patriot groups in Charleston, New York, and Pennsylvania had been able to convince the consignees (persons in charge of the tea) to return to London without unloading the tea. However, in Boston, neither the consignees, nor the customs collector, nor the governor would agree to do this.

Sam Adams sent Francis Rotch, owner of two of the ships, to try one more time to convince the governor to allow the ships to go back to London with the tea. When he returned, he informed Adams that the governor had once again refused to negotiate with them. Adams rose and exclaimed, "This meeting can do nothing more to save this country."

Destruction of the Tea

That night hundreds of colonists dressed in the manner of Mohawk Indians and boarded the ships. They dumped 340 chests—more than 92,000 pounds—of tea into the water. The protest was not violent. Except for the chests of tea, no property was destroyed, and nothing was stolen.

About a week later, another, smaller protest took place in Philadelphia. A group of colonists intercepted a British tea ship and forced it to return to Britain without unloading its cargo.

In reaction to the destruction of the tea, the British shut down Boston Harbor and refused to reopen it until the colonists paid for the tea. Parliament also passed several acts known collectively as the Coercive Acts. The Coercive Acts comprised the Boston Port Act and the Quarting Act among others. Outraged by these measures, the colonists responded by convening the First Continental Congress. The Congress met in September and October 1774. They petitioned the British government to repeal these acts, which they called the Intolerable Acts.

The Boston Tea Party, known at the time as "The Destruction of the Tea," was the first planned and executed act of rebellion by the colonists against Britain. It was a non-violent protest, but the unrest was not over, and that unrest would lead in the not-too-distant future to America's War for Independence.

Monday Morning, December 27, 1773.

THE Tea-Ship being arrived, every Inhabitant who wishes to preserve the Liberty of America, is desired to meet at the STATE-HOUSE, This Morning, precisely at TEN o'Clock, to advise what is best to be done on this alarming Crisis.

SOURCE: Library of Congress

Americans throwing the Cargoes of the Tea Ships into the River, at Boston

By W.D. Cooper. "Boston Tea Party"

Think About It: Broadside

1. Where, do you think, was the broadside on the previous page published? Use the background information to it figure out.

2. What was the purpose of the notice?

3. According to the writer of the notice, why was it important that people meet at the arranged time?

Think About It: Engraving

1. Some historians believe that when Sam Adams exclaimed, "This meeting can do nothing more to save this country," it was a signal. Knowing what followed, do you agree? Explain.

2. Sam Adams and other leaders stayed at the meeting house after most of the attendees departed. In your opinion, why did they do this?

3. The colonists called the acts passed by Britain in response to the destruction of the tea "The Coercive Acts." The colonists called them "The Intolerable Acts." How did each name reflect the point of view of the user?

4. What does the engraving on the previous page tell us about how some colonists dressed for the event?

5. What are the men aboard the ship doing?

6. One of the men on the ship is using a tool. Why, do you think, did the colonists bring tools like this one on board the ships?

7. What does the illustration tell us about whether or not there were witnesses to the "Tea Party"?

Patrick Henry
"Give Me Liberty or Give Me Death"

Background Information

On March 20, 1775, the Second Virginia Convention met in Richmond, Virginia. The president of the convention was Peyton Randolph of Williamsburg. Several of the delegates presented their point of view regarding their growing unrest. Some called for continued patience and urged the delegates to wait for Britain's response to the Continental Congress's attempt at reconciliation. Patrick Henry held a different view. On March 23 he urged Virginians to form a militia and to ready themselves for defense against Great Britain. His closing line—"Give me liberty, or give me death!"—is among the best known quotations of all time.

Patrick Henry did not write down his speech, and it was not transcribed at the time it was given. It wasn't until 1808, nine years after Henry's death, that William Wirt of Maryland began to interview those who had been present to reconstruct a speech close to the one given by Patrick Henry on that memorable day.

By George Bagby Matthews (1857–1943), Copy of Portrait by Thomas Sully (1783–1872)

William Wirt's Reconstruction of
"Give Me Liberty, or Give Me Death! Speech"

MR. PRESIDENT: No man thinks more highly than I do of the patriotism, as well as abilities, of the very worthy gentlemen who have just addressed the House. But different men often see the same subject in different lights; and, therefore, I hope it will not be thought disrespectful to those gentlemen if, entertaining as I do, opinions of a character very opposite to theirs, I shall speak forth my sentiments freely, and without reserve. This is no time for ceremony. The question before the House is one of awful moment to this country. For my own part, I consider it as nothing less than a question of freedom or slavery; and in proportion to the magnitude of the subject ought to be the freedom of the debate. It is only in this way that we can hope to arrive at truth, and fulfil the great responsibility which we hold to God and our country. Should I keep back my opinions at such a time, through fear of giving offence, I should consider myself as guilty of treason towards my country, and of an act of disloyalty toward the majesty of heaven, which I revere above all earthly kings.

Mr. President, it is natural to man to indulge in the illusions of hope. We are apt to shut our eyes against a painful truth, and listen to the song of that siren till she transforms us into beasts. Is this the part of wise men, engaged in a great and arduous struggle for liberty? Are we disposed to be of the number of those who, having eyes, see not, and, having ears, hear not, the things which so nearly concern their temporal salvation? For my part, whatever anguish of spirit it may cost, I am willing to know the whole truth; to know the worst, and to provide for it.

I have but one lamp by which my feet are guided; and that is the lamp of experience. I know of no way of judging of the future but by the past. And judging by the past, I wish to know what there has been in the conduct of the British ministry for the last ten years, to justify those hopes with which gentlemen have been pleased to solace themselves, and the House? Is it that insidious smile with which our petition has been lately received? Trust it not, sir; it will prove a snare to your feet. Suffer not yourselves to be betrayed with a kiss. Ask yourselves how this gracious reception of our petition comports with these war-like preparations which cover our waters and darken our land. Are fleets and armies necessary to a work of love and reconciliation? Have we shown ourselves so unwilling to be reconciled, that force must be called in to win back our love? Let us not deceive ourselves, sir. These are the implements of war and subjugation; the last arguments to which kings resort. I ask, gentlemen, sir, what means this martial array, if its purpose be not to force us to submission? Can gentlemen assign any other possible motive for it?

Has Great Britain any enemy, in this quarter of the world, to call for all this accumulation of navies and armies? No, sir, she has none. They are meant for us; they can be meant for no other. They are sent over to bind and rivet upon us those chains which the British ministry have been so long forging. And what have we to oppose to them? Shall we try argument? Sir, we have been trying that for the last ten years. Have we anything new to offer upon the subject? Nothing. We have held the subject up in every light of which it is capable; but it has been all in vain. Shall we resort to entreaty and humble supplication? What terms shall we find which have not been already exhausted? Let us not, I beseech you, sir, deceive ourselves. Sir, we have done everything that could be done, to avert the storm which is now coming on. We have petitioned; we have remonstrated; we have supplicated; we have prostrated ourselves before the throne, and have implored its interposition to arrest the tyrannical hands of the ministry and Parliament. Our petitions have been slighted; our remonstrances have produced additional violence and insult; our supplications have been disregarded; and we have been spurned, with contempt, from the foot of the throne. In vain, after these things, may we indulge the fond hope of peace and reconciliation. There is no longer any room for hope. If we wish to be free, if we mean to preserve inviolate those inestimable privileges for which we have been so long contending, if we mean not basely to abandon the noble struggle in which we have been so long engaged, and which we have pledged ourselves never to abandon until the glorious object of our contest shall be obtained, we must fight! I repeat it, sir, we must fight! An appeal to arms and to the God of Hosts is all that is left us!

They tell us, sir, that we are weak; unable to cope with so formidable an adversary. But when shall we be stronger? Will it be the next week, or the next year? Will it be when we are totally disarmed, and when a British guard shall be stationed in every house? Shall we gather strength by irresolution and inaction? Shall we acquire the means of effectual resistance, by lying supinely on our backs, and hugging the delusive phantom of hope, until our enemies shall have bound us hand and foot? Sir, we are not weak if we make a proper use of those means which the God of nature hath placed in our power. Three millions of people, armed in the holy cause of liberty, and in such a country as that which we possess, are invincible by any force which our enemy can send against us. Besides, sir, we shall not fight our battles alone. There is a just God who presides over the destinies of nations; and who will raise up friends to fight our battles for us. The battle, sir, is not to the strong alone; it is to the vigilant, the active, the brave. Besides, sir, we have no election. If we were base enough to desire it, it is now too late to retire from the contest. There is no retreat but in submission and slavery! Our chains are forged! Their clanking may be heard on the plains of Boston! The war is inevitable, and let it come! I repeat it, sir, let it come.

It is in vain, sir, to extenuate the matter. Gentlemen may cry, Peace, Peace, but there is no peace. The war is actually begun! The next gale that sweeps from the north will bring to our ears the clash of resounding arms! Our brethren are already in the field! Why stand we here idle? What is it that gentlemen wish? What would they have? Is life so dear, or peace so sweet, as to be purchased at the price of chains and slavery? Forbid it, Almighty God! I know not what course others may take; but as for me, give me liberty or give me death!

Think About It

1. Analyze the first two paragraphs of the speech. What was Henry's attitude towards those who disagreed with his point of view? Cite examples. Do you think that maintaining this attitude helped him win them over to his side?

2. What function did the first two paragraphs serve?

3. Do you think that Patrick Henry was smart not to put the speech in writing? Explain.

4. The use of the word "awful" in sentence 4 is different from the way the word is commonly used today. What is the meaning as used in this sentence?

5. Henry used many biblical allusions. In the second paragraph of the speech he also included an allusion to mythical creatures of Greek mythology. Find that allusion and explain its use here.

6. Whom is Henry addressing when he says, "Mr. President"?

7. In the fourth paragraph of the speech Patrick Henry emphasized the fact that the colonists had done all they could to maintain peace. What verbs did he use to enumerate all the steps they had taken?

Currier & Ives Depiction of Henry Giving His Famous Speech
SOURCE: Library of Congress

8. Metonymy is a metaphor that substitutes something associated with a thing for the name of that thing. For example, we often refer to the President as the White House. Henry said, "We have prostrated ourselves before the throne." Rewrite the sentence without the use of metonymy.

9. "Give me liberty or give me death" is an example of an either-or fallacy. Explain what that means and why this type of fallacy is often used in propaganda.

10. What is the setting of this visual? How do you know?

11. What does the Currier & Ives print tell us about the reaction of the others present?

Thomas Paine
Common Sense

Background Information

Thomas Paine is probably the best known pamphleteer of the eighteenth century. In addition to *Common Sense,* he wrote *The Rights of Man* and *The Age of Reason.* When *Common Sense* was published in January 1776, there was already a great deal of unrest in the colonies. However, in spite of their concern about many of the actions taken by the British, many of the colonists were not ready to declare independence from Britain.

Thomas Paine was convinced that breaking away from Britain was inevitable and he used *Common Sense* to convince others of this necessity. In it he wrote against the fact that the monarchy's authority was based only on heredity. He stated his belief that citizens should have a say in government. Paine also wrote convincingly of the colonies' need to band together and of the importance of America's readiness to fight Britain for independence.

Common Sense was an immediate success. More than 500,000 copies were sold in the first year—about 120,000 in the three months. It was an important factor in convincing many that the time for independence had come. Indeed, it was no coincidence that the Declaration of Independence was signed only six months after the publication of the pamphlet.

Reproduction of George Romney's Engraving, by William Sharp

Think About It: Cover of *Common Sense*

1. Study the cover of *Common Sense,* shown on page 27. Who was the intended audience for the pamphlet?

2. Where and by whom was the pamphlet published?

3. In what year was it published?

4. What are the four "subjects" addressed in the pamphlet? How are they organized?

5. Can you infer whose copy this is?

Common Sense Excerpts...

Excerpt #1: From "Of the Origin and Design of Government in General, with Concise Remarks on the English Constitution"

SOME writers have so confounded society with government, as to leave little or no distinction between them; whereas they are not only different, but have different origins. Society is produced by our wants, and government by our wickedness; the former promotes our happiness POSITIVELY by uniting our affections, the latter NEGATIVELY by restraining our vices. ...

Society in every state is a blessing, but Government, even in its best state, is but a necessary evil; in its worst state an intolerable one: for when we suffer, or are exposed to the same miseries BY A GOVERNMENT, which we might expect in a country WITHOUT GOVERNMENT, our calamity is heightened by reflecting that we furnish the means by which we suffer. Government, like dress, is the badge of lost innocence; the palaces of kings are built upon the ruins of the bowers of paradise. For were the impulses of conscience clear, uniform and irresistibly obeyed, man would need no other lawgiver; but that not being the case, he finds it necessary to surrender up a part of his property to furnish means for the protection of the rest; and this he is induced to do by the same prudence which in every other case advises him, out of two evils to choose the least. Wherefore, security being the true design and end of government, it unanswerably follows that whatever form thereof appears most likely to ensure it to us, with the least expense and greatest benefit, is preferable to all others.

Excerpt #2: From "Of Monarchy and Hereditary Succession"

But there is another and great distinction for which no truly natural or religious reason can be assigned, and that is the distinction of men into KINGS and SUBJECTS. Male and female are the distinctions of nature, good and bad the distinctions of Heaven; but how a race of men came into the world so exalted above the rest, and distinguished like some new species, is worth inquiring into, and whether they are the means of happiness or of misery to mankind....

But it is not so much the absurdity as the evil of hereditary succession which concerns mankind. Did it ensure a race of good and wise men it would have the seal of divine authority, but as it opens a door to the FOOLISH, the WICKED, and the IMPROPER, it hath in it the nature of oppression. Men who look upon themselves born to reign, and others to obey, soon grow insolent. Selected from the rest of mankind, their minds are early poisoned by importance; and the world they act in differs so materially from the world at large, that they have but little opportunity of knowing its true interests, and when they succeed in the government are frequently the most ignorant and unfit of any throughout the dominions.

Excerpt #3: From "Thoughts on the Present State of American Affairs"

I challenge the warmest advocate for reconciliation to show a single advantage that this continent can reap by being connected with Great Britain. I repeat the challenge; not a single advantage is derived. Our corn will fetch its price in any market in Europe, and our imported goods must be paid for buy them where we will.

But the injuries and disadvantages which we sustain by that connection, are without number; and our duty to mankind at large, as well as to ourselves, instruct us to renounce the alliance: because, any submission to, or dependence on, Great Britain, tends directly to involve this Continent in European wars and quarrels, and set us at variance with nations who would otherwise seek our friendship, and against whom we have neither anger nor complaint. As Europe is our market for trade, we ought to form no partial connection with any part of it. It is the true interest of America to steer clear of European contentions, which she never can do, while, by her dependence on Britain, she is made the makeweight in the scale of British politics.

Excerpt #4: From "Of the Present Ability of America: with some Miscellaneous Reflections"

'Tis not in numbers but in unity that our great strength lies: yet our present numbers are sufficient to repel the force of all the world. The Continent hath at this time the largest body of armed and disciplined men of any power under Heaven: and is just arrived at that pitch of strength, in which no single colony is able to support itself, and the whole, when united, is able to do any thing. Our land force is more than sufficient, and as to Naval affairs, we cannot be insensible that Britain would never suffer an American man of war to be built, while the Continent remained in her hands. Wherefore, we should be no forwarder an hundred years hence in that branch than we are now; but the truth is, we should be less so, because the timber of the Country is every day diminishing, and that which will remain at last, will be far off or difficult to procure....

Youth is the seed-time of good habits as well in nations as in individuals. It might be difficult, if not impossible, to form the Continent into one government half a century hence. The vast variety of interests, occasioned by an increase of trade and population, would create confusion. Colony would be against colony. Each being able would scorn each other's assistance; and while the proud and foolish gloried in their little distinctions the wise would lament that the union had not been formed before. Wherefore the present time is the true time for establishing it. ...

Think About It: Excerpts
Read the excerpts on the previous page and then answer these questions.

1. According to Paine, how do government and society differ? (Excerpt #1)

2. Describe Paine's general view of government. How should government be judged? (Excerpt #1)

3. What are Paine's views on the monarchy and hereditary succession? (Excerpt #2)

4. According to Paine, what was the result of hereditary succession? (Excerpt #2)

By Thomas Paine

5. What was Paine's response to those who said that America had flourished under British rule? (Excerpt #3)

6. According to Paine, why were those who argued that the colonies were too small to defeat Britain wrong? (Excerpt #4)

© Barbara M. Peller

The Declaration of Independence
When in the Course of Human Events...

Background Information

The conflicts of the Revolutionary War began in April 1775 in Massachusetts at the Battles of Lexington and Concord. At that time, most colonists were fighting for their rights but not for independence. During the next year, however, the desire for independence grew, and on June 7, 1776, the Continental Congress, with John Hancock as its president, met in Philadelphia at the Pennsylvania State House, later called Independence Hall.

Richard Henry Lee introduced a motion to call for independence, and an impassioned debate followed. The vote on Lee's motion was postponed, and Congress called for a recess to give the delegates time to think about what had been discussed. Before the delegates left, however, Congress appointed a committee to draft a document giving reasons to break with Great Britain. The five members of the committee were John Adams of Massachusetts, Benjamin Franklin of Pennsylvania, Thomas Jefferson of Virginia, Robert R. Livingston of New York, and Roger Sherman of Connecticut.

Because of his reputation as an outstanding writer, the other members insisted that Thomas Jefferson create the document. Jefferson accepted. He wrote the Declaration of Independence, dividing the document into five sections: an introduction, a preamble, a 2-part body, and a conclusion. When done, he sent his rough copy to Benjamin Franklin and John Adams and asked them to make corrections before he showed it to the others in the committee and then to Congress.

On July 1 the Continental Congress reconvened, and on July 2 all of the colonies except New York adopted Richard Lee's resolution calling for independence. The delegates spent the next two days editing the Declaration, but the Preamble remained as Jefferson had written it. On July 4 the Declaration of Independence was adopted, but it was not signed until August 2.

By John Trumbull

Think About It:
John Trumbull Painting

1. Study the painting by John Trumbull. Use what you read in the Background Information to infer who the five men standing in front of the table are.

2. Now infer who is seated at the table, about to receive the document.

In Congress, July 4, 1776.

The unanimous Declaration of the thirteen united States of America.

[Full handwritten text of the Declaration of Independence, followed by the signatures of the signers including John Hancock, Button Gwinnett, Lyman Hall, Geo Walton, Wm Hooper, Joseph Hewes, John Penn, Edward Rutledge, Thos Heyward Junr, Thomas Lynch Junr, Arthur Middleton, Samuel Chase, Wm Paca, Thos Stone, Charles Carroll of Carrollton, George Wythe, Richard Henry Lee, Th Jefferson, Benj Harrison, Ths Nelson jr, Francis Lightfoot Lee, Carter Braxton, Robt Morris, Benjamin Rush, Benj Franklin, John Morton, Geo Clymer, Jas Smith, Geo Taylor, James Wilson, Geo Ross, Caesar Rodney, Geo Read, Tho M:Kean, Wm Floyd, Phil Livingston, Frans Lewis, Lewis Morris, Richd Stockton, Jno Witherspoon, Fras Hopkinson, John Hart, Abra Clark, Josiah Bartlett, Wm Whipple, Saml Adams, John Adams, Robt Treat Paine, Elbridge Gerry, Step Hopkins, William Ellery, Roger Sherman, Samel Huntington, Wm Williams, Oliver Wolcott, Matthew Thornton]

TRANSCRIPTION OF THE PREAMBLE AND INTRODUCTION

When in the Course of human events it becomes necessary for one people to dissolve the political bands which have connected them with another and to assume among the powers of the earth, the separate and equal station to which the Laws of Nature and of Nature's God entitle them, a decent respect to the opinions of mankind requires that they should declare the causes which impel them to the separation.

We hold these truths to be self-evident, that all men are created equal, that they are endowed by their Creator with certain unalienable Rights, that among these are Life, Liberty and the pursuit of Happiness. — That to secure these rights, Governments are instituted among Men, deriving their just powers from the consent of the governed, — That whenever any Form of Government becomes destructive of these ends, it is the Right of the People to alter or to abolish it, and to institute new Government, laying its foundation on such principles and organizing its powers in such form, as to them shall seem most likely to effect their Safety and Happiness. Prudence, indeed, will dictate that Governments long established should not be changed for light and transient causes; and accordingly all experience hath shewn that mankind are more disposed to suffer, while evils are sufferable than to right themselves by abolishing the forms to which they are accustomed. But when a long train of abuses and usurpations, pursuing invariably the same Object evinces a design to reduce them under absolute Despotism, it is their right, it is their duty, to throw off such Government, and to provide new Guards for their future security. — Such has been the patient sufferance of these Colonies; and such is now the necessity which constrains them to alter their former Systems of Government. The history of the present King of Great Britain is a history of repeated injuries and usurpations, all having in direct object the establishment of an absolute Tyranny over these States. To prove this, let Facts be submitted to a candid world.

TRANSCRIPTION OF AN EXCERPT FROM THE BODY

He has kept among us, in times of peace, Standing Armies without the Consent of our legislatures.

He has affected to render the Military independent of and superior to the Civil power.

He has combined with others to subject us to a jurisdiction foreign to our constitution, and unacknowledged by our laws; giving his Assent to their Acts of pretended Legislation.

For Quartering large bodies of armed troops among us:

For protecting them, by a mock Trial, from punishment for any Murders which they should commit on the Inhabitants of these States:

For cutting off our Trade with all parts of the world:

For imposing Taxes on us without our Consent:

For depriving us in many cases, of the benefits of Trial by Jury:

For transporting us beyond Seas to be tried for pretended offences:

LAST PARAGRAPH OF THE CONCLUSION

We, therefore, the Representatives of the united States of America, in General Congress, Assembled, appealing to the Supreme Judge of the world for the rectitude of our intentions, do, in the Name, and by Authority of the good People of these Colonies, solemnly publish and declare, That these United Colonies are, and of Right ought to be Free and Independent States; that they are Absolved from all Allegiance to the British Crown, and that all political connection between them and the State of Great Britain, is and ought to be totally dissolved; and that as Free and Independent States, they have full Power to levy War, conclude Peace, contract Alliances, establish Commerce, and to do all other Acts and Things which Independent States may of right do. And for the support of this Declaration, with a firm reliance on the protection of divine Providence, we mutually pledge to each other our Lives, our Fortunes and our sacred Honor.

Think About It: Excerpts from Document

1. The Preamble states the reason for the document. What is that reason?

2. What are the inevitable truths mentioned in the Introduction?

3. According to the Introduction, what is government's role?

4. From the excerpt given, infer the purpose of the body of the document.

5. Read the last paragraph of the conclusion. What is the significance of the following regarding the future of the United States of America: "That these United Colonies are, and of Right ought to be Free and Independent States; that they are Absolved from all Allegiance to the British Crown, and that all political connection between them and the State of Great Britain, is and ought to be totally dissolved; and that as Free and Independent States, they have full Power to levy War, conclude Peace, contract Alliances, establish Commerce, and to do all other Acts and Things which Independent States may of right do"?

6. In spite of the fact that they were declaring themselves independent states, what would their relationship be to one another?

Burgoyne's Surrender at Saratoga
Turning Point of the War

Background Information

Early in the summer of 1777 General John Burgoyne put into action his plan to march south from Canada with his troops through the Hudson Valley to Albany, New York. His army of about 7,000 men comprised about an equal number of British and Hessians, German troops hired by the British to help them fight the Americans. The ultimate goal was to divide the Americans by cutting off New England from the other colonies. Burgoyne's plan depended upon being met with reinforcements under General Howe, who was to march north with troops from New York and New Jersey. The British did win some campaigns along the way, but his strategy did not go as planned.

In August Burgoyne sent German troops to Vermont to capture the supply depot in Bennington. He had received word that the depot was lightly guarded and could be easily taken. However, American general John Stark and his men were able to capture the 500 Hessians. One of the reasons for their failure to carry out their mission was that the hundreds of Tories, or Loyalists, expected by Burgoyne to come to their assistance, never arrived.

Surrender of General John Burgoyne to General Horatio Gates
by John Trumbull
The original painting is on display in the Rotunda of the U.S. Capitol.

On September 19 General Burgoyne and his troops were met by American forces led by General Horatio Gates at Freeman's Farm, which was north of Albany. The battle that followed became known as the First Battle of Saratoga. The British were victorious, but at great cost in terms of the number of men lost in the battle.

On October 7 General Gates, General Burgoyne, and theirs troops met once again, this time at Bemis Heights, south of Saratoga. General Burgoyne's original plan was to be met by reinforcements led by General Howe; however, instead of marching north to meet Burgoyne, General Howe took his troops on a campaign to capture Philadelphia.

The Battle at Bemis Heights, called the Second Battle of Saratoga, ended in a demoralizing defeat for the British. Nine days later—on October 17—5,895 British and Hessian troops surrendered their arms to General Burgoyne.

Many historians consider the decisive victory at Saratoga the turning point of the American Revolution. Other nations began to believe that the Americans might actually succeed in their attempt to win their independence from Great Britain. It was this factor that led to France's decision to aid the Americans both financially and militarily. That assistance would prove invaluable to the Americans.

Think About It

1. Which man in the painting is General Burgoyne? How do you know?

2. Which man is General Gates? How do you know?

3. The man being offered the sword does not appear to be taking it. What does this tell us?

4. The man in the center appears to be pointing. To what is he pointing?

5. The way the men are dressed reflects their different units, but the man standing five to the right of the man in the center is dressed differently from all the others. Can you guess why?

6. Describe the mood that the painting conveys.

NOTE: The names of the men in the painting are listed left to right in the answer section.

© Barbara M. Peller

Spies in the American Revolution
Benedict Arnold

Background Information

Benedict Arnold, whose name is now synonymous with "traitor," at one time fought for the American cause. As early as May 19, 1775, he joined forces with Ethan Allan's Green Mountain Boys and led a regiment that captured Fort Ticonderoga in New York.

Arnold drew the attention of General Washington, who gave him command of a band of troops and ordered him to lead those troops in an attack of Quebec. Washington also wanted Arnold to convince the Canadians to rally behind the Americans. The aim was to prevent the British from using Canada as a base from which to attack. Arnold launched his attack on December 31, 1775, during a blizzard. He suffered a serious leg wound during the battle and had to be carried off the battlefield. The Americans lost the battle, and the British continued to control Canada.

When his wound healed sufficiently, Arnold again fought for the Patriots. He correctly predicted that the British general Guy Caleton planned to sail with a fleet from Canada to invade New York and arranged for an American flotilla to meet the British at Lake Champlain. That flotilla surprised Carleton's fleet on October 11, 1776. Although the British were not stopped, they were delayed long enough so that when they finally reached New York, it was too late to carry out their plan. Because the winter months were approaching, the New York battle season was over. Carleton's fleet had no choice but to return to Canada.

It was about this time that Arnold began to resent the way he was being treated. His heroic actions basically went unnoticed. To make matters worse, in 1777 five officers who had been below him in rank were promoted above him. Disillusioned, he resigned from the Continental Army.

General Washington convinced Arnold to rejoin, and in October 1777 Arnold took part in the battles of Saratoga, which were fought in defense of New York. The British troops were led by General John Burgoyne; American troops were led by General Horatio Gates. Gates and Arnold had a mutual dislike, and Gates relieved Arnold of his command at the Battle of Bemis Heights, also known as the first Battle of Saratoga. Arnold defied Gates and led a group of soldiers against the British line. This action was a major reason for the Americans' success at Saratoga, but Gates was furious. In his reports, he minimized Arnold's contribution and took credit for the victory. To add to Arnold's discontent, he was wounded in the same leg he had previously injured. This injury made him temporarily unable to have a field command.

General Washington appointed him military governor of Philadelphia. While in Philadelphia, Arnold married Peggy Shippen, whose father was a suspected Loyalist. The couple lived extravagantly and built up quite a large debt. Many people believed that he was using his office for personal gain and accused him of corruption. Arnold resigned his Philadelphia command on March 19, 1779.

Arnold's feelings of resentment grew and he began to carry out acts of treason against the Americans. This behavior came to a climax in the summer of 1780. Arnold was in command of West Point, a fort on the Hudson River in New York. He contacted Sir Henry Clinton and conspired with him to have the Americans at West Point surrender to the British. Arnold asked Clinton for 20,000 pounds in return.

In August Arnold got word that Clinton had accepted his offer. Major John André and Benedict Arnold negotiated their agreement, and on September 19, Clinton prepared to capture the fort. However, on September 23 André was captured. His captors found the papers he was carrying with information about West Point's garrisons and defenses. They also found a pass that Arnold had provided. The plot arranged by Benedict Arnold had failed, and André was later hanged as a spy by the Continental Army.

Arnold's treachery was now known by all. He joined the British forces as a brigadier and fought against American forces in New York and in Virginia. When General Cornwallis returned to England after the British surrendered at Yorktown, Arnold and his family sailed with him. In spite of the fact that he once fought heroically for the Patriots, he will always be remembered for his treasonous actions.

Source: The National Archives

Think About It

1. What is the above document?

2. What was Arnold's rank upon signing?

3. When did he sign it?

4. How did he betray it?

5. What did Arnold write in the blank space? Why, do you think, was the space left blank?

6. H. Knox witnessed this signing. Research and find out what future role he would play.

Spies in the American Revolution
Techniques

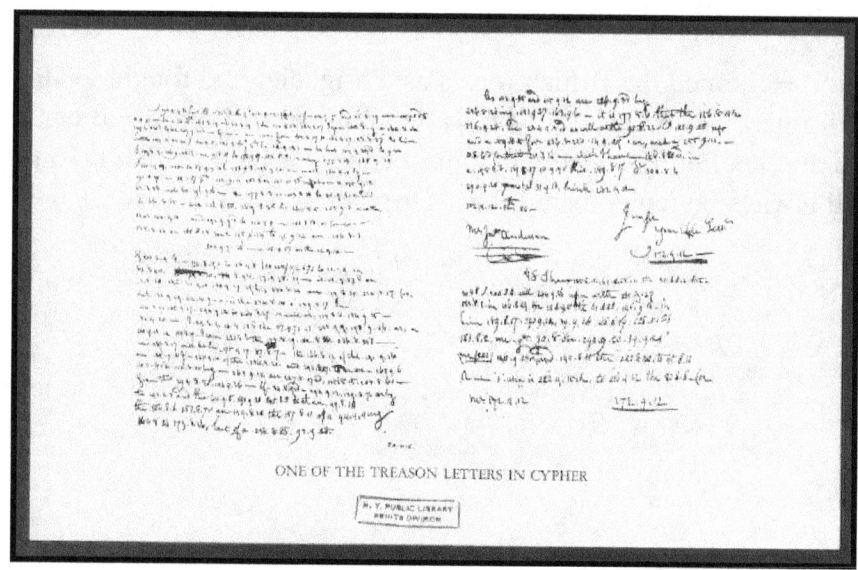

ONE OF THE TREASON LETTERS IN CYPHER

Source: New York Public Library

INVISIBLE INK
Both the British and the American armies used invisible ink to send secret messages. Benedict Arnold inserted coded text using invisible ink among the lines of text written by his wife in the letter to the left. His intent was to communicate with the British while negotiating the surrender of the fort at West Point.

MASKING
The British used masks such as the one below to be placed over the complete letter. The text that remained uncovered supplied secret information to the recipient of the letter.

TRANSCRIPTIONS OF A LETTER, MASKED AND UNMASKED, FROM BRITISH ARMY OFFICER SIR HENRY CLINTON TO BRITISH GENERAL JOHN BURGOYNE

Without Mask
You will have heard, Dr Sir I doubt not long before this can have reached you that Sir W. Howe is gone from hence. The Rebels imagine that he is gone to the Eastward. By this time however he has filled Chesapeake bay with surprize and terror.

Washington marched the greater part of the Rebels to Philadelphia in order to oppose Sir Wm's. army. I hear he is now returned upon finding none of our troops landed but am not sure of this, great part of his troops are returned for certain. I am sure this countermarching must be ruin to them. I am left to command here, half of my force may I am sure defend everything here with much safety. I shall therefore send Sir W. 4 or 5 Bat [talio] ns. I have too small a force to invade the New England provinces; they are too weak to make any effectual efforts against me and you do not want any diversion in your favour. I can, therefore very well spare him 1500 men. I shall try some thing certainly towards the close of the year, not till then at any rate. It may be of use to inform you that report says all yields to you. I own to you that I think the business will quickly be over now. Sr. W's move just at this time has been capital. Wahingtons have been the worst he could take in every respect. sincerely give you much joy on your success and am with great Sincerity your (?)

With Mask
Sir. W. Howe is gone to the Chesapeak bay with the greatest part of the army. I hear he is landed but am not certain. I am left to command here with too small a force to make any effectual diversion in your favour. I shall try something at any rate. It may be of use to you. I own to you I think Sr W's move just at this time the worst he could take. Much joy on your success.

	A	34	assign	67	barron
1	a	35	assume	68	brigade
2	an	36	attempt	69	business
3	all	37	attone	70	battery
4	at	38	attack	71	battallion
5	and	39	alarm	72	British
6	art	40	action		C
7	arms	41	accomplish	73	camp
8	about	42	apprehend	74	came
9	above	43	abatis	75	cost
10	absent	44	accomodate	76	corps
11	absurd	45	alternative	77	change
12	adorn	46	artillery	78	carry
13	adopt	47	ammunition	79	clergy
14	adore		B	80	common
15	advise	48	be	81	consult
16	adjust	49	bay	82	contest
17	adjourn	50	by	83	contract
18	afford	51	best	84	content
19	affront	52	but	85	Congress
20	affair	53	buy	86	captain
21	again	54	bring	87	careful
22	April	55	boat	88	city
23	agent	56	barn	89	clamour
24	alter	57	banish	90	column
25	ally	58	baker	91	copy
26	any	59	battle	92	cover
27	appear	60	better	93	county
28	appoint	61	beacon	94	courage
29	August	62	behalf	95	credit
30	approve	63	bitter	96	custom
31	arrest	64	bottom	97	compute
32	arraign	65	bounty	98	conduct
33	amuse	66	bondage	99	comply

On the left is a reproduction of the first page of the Culper Code Book. On the right is a list of the first 99 words in the book.

THE CULPER CODE BOOK

At the request of General Washington, in 1778 Major Benjamin Tallmadge organized what became known as the Culper Spy Ring. Its purpose was to obtain information about the troop movements, fortifications, and battle plans of British troops in the New York region. Members of the spy ring used fake names and a numerical code book consisting of seven hundred and sixty-three numbers. Those numbers represented not only letters, numbers, and words, but also important names and places.

Think About It

1. What was the purpose of ciphers and secret codes?

2. Research invisible ink. Explain how the recipient was able to retrieve the secret information.

3. Analyze the importance to General Washington of the intelligence acquired through secret correspondence.

4. How do you think the senders of masked letters dealt with the problem of the mask being used by the enemy to interpret the secret message?

Valley Forge
The Harsh Winter of 1777–1778

Background Information

As the winter of 1777 approached, things looked bad for General Washington and the Continental Army. Morale was down after their losses at the Brandywine and Germantown, Pennsylvania. Some members of the Continental Congress had begun to question Washington's ability as a leader. When Washington defied Congress's order to attack the British, their relationship worsened.

The British had occupied Philadelphia, and it was clear they intended to remain there for the winter. Congress wanted Washington to attack, but instead he decided to fall back with his 12,000 men to Valley Forge, about 18 miles northwest of Philadelphia. From there Washington could monitor the movements of the British and could prevent them from using the area to obtain food. Washington and his men arrived at Valley Forge on December 19, 1777.

Baron Steuben by Peale, 1780
Charles Willson Peale

Conditions at Valley Forge were extremely harsh. There was no shelter for the troops, so huts had to be built. Food was scarce, and the men were in dire need of warm clothing, blankets, boots, and other supplies. Typhoid, dysentery, pneumonia, and other diseases spread throughout the encampment. Some estimates put the death toll at Valley Forge at more than 2,000.

Despite Washington's pleas, at first the Continental Congress refused to provide the needed provisions. About a month after their arrival, however, Congress sent a delegation of five men to investigate the conditions at Valley Forge. When they saw how dire the situation was, they reported their findings, and Congress began to send the much-needed supplies.

Many of the men's wives and children also encamped at Valley Forge. Martha Washington arrived on February 10. She organized a sewing circle, where the women knitted socks and mended clothing for the men. Some of the women helped by serving as nurses and laundresses.

On February 23, something happened that would turn things around for Washington and his men. General Friedrich von Steuben, a Prussian general, arrived with a letter of introduction from Benjamin Franklin, whom he had met in France. Steuben volunteered to train Washington's undisciplined troops. Washington readily accepted the offer.

Washington appointed Steuben as inspector general, and Steuben immediately got to work. One of the first things he did was to separate the men into squads so he could train them one squad at a time. He also took measures to improve sanitary practices in order to reduce the spread of disease. Steuben's native language was German and he spoke no English. He gave his orders in German or French and relied on assistants to translate. His efforts were successful. He turned a raggedy bunch of undisciplined men into disciplined, well-trained troops prepared for battle.

38 *Using Primary Sources to Teach U.S. History: War to Constitution* © **Barbara M. Peller**

In May 1778 General Washington and his men received the welcome news that because of the Americans' victory at Saratoga, France had formally agreed to aid the Americans. When they left Valley Forge a few weeks later on June 19—exactly six months after their arrival—they left as an optimistic, cohesive army.

On June 19, 1778, the British left Philadelphia and headed for New York City. Washington and his men followed in pursuit and met them at Monmouth Courthouse, New Jersey. Neither side could claim a clear victory, but the American forces showed that they were now a serious fighting force.

Think About It

Study the letter and its transcription on the next page and then respond to these questions:

1. Who wrote the letter? What was his position?

2. To whom was the letter written? Where was that person located?

3. When was the letter sent?

4. What was the purpose of the letter?

5. On the cover and near the end of the letter it says, "On publick Service." What does that mean?

6. Where will the supplies be sent?

Baron von Steuben Drilling Troops at Valley Forge
by E. A. Abbey (c.1904)

TRANSCRIPTION OF THE LETTER

Nathanael Greene to Joseph Webb, 1778
Camp. Valley Forge, 2d of April 1778
Sir

    In order to lessen the Quantity of Baggage in the Army &enable it to move with the greater Ease, it is proposed to lay aside as much as possible, the Use of Chests and Trunks: A large Number of Portmanteaus and Valeeses is therefore become necessary for the Officers; and as I am informed some of these may be collected in Connecticut, I request the Favour of you to procure as many good leather Portmanteaus, of about the middling Size, as can be got ready to send forward by or before the middle of May—the Number I shall expect from you will be about 200. at least; and 20, or 30 Valeeses for Matrasses to be made of pretty strong Canvas. If you can meet with any Canvas, Ticklenburgs and Oznaburgs suitable for Tents, Knapsacks &c, I should be glad you would purchase it for me. As fast as you can collect any of these Articles in any considerable Quantity, be pleased to forward them to the Care of Mr. Hugh Hughes, D. Qur. Master at Fishkill who will send them on to Camp.

    I expect in very short Time to remit you Money sufficient to pay for the Articles you may purchase, so that I think you may rely on being enabled to make punctual Payments, which I doubt not will not only facilitate the Business but enable you to do it on better Terms than it could otherwise be done. In the mean Time I beg you will inform me what Quantity of these articles are likely to be procured in Connecticut within the Time I have mentioned, and that you will give me the speediest Information when any Goods shall be sent forward.

    I rely on your Zeal in the Publick Service to take upon you this Trouble, and to employ such Persons in the Business, as you shall think most likely to effect it to the best Advantage & with the greatest Dispatch, allowing them such Compensation as you shall think reasonable; and for your own Troubles, besides your Expences of which be pleased to make a Charge, you will be allowed a Commission adequate to the Business.

    I take it for granted you have been informed of my Appointment to the Office of Quarter-Master-General of the Army of the the [sic] United States, and it is in that Character I now apply to you.

    I am, with Regard, Sir,
        Your most obedient humble Servant
            Nathel Greene
            Q M General

To Joseph Webb Esqr.
Weathersfield

Cover and Letter from Camp Valley Forge

Gilbert du Motier, Marquis de Lafayette
French Military Officer

Background Information

Known simply as Lafayette, at the age of nineteen Marquis de Lafayette voluntarily joined the Continental Army as a Major General to come to the aid of the American revolutionaries. The first battle in which he fought was the Battle of Brandywine, Pennsylvania. Lafayette was wounded, and the Patriots were forced to retreat; nevertheless, Lafayette managed to organize the retreat and get his men to safety. For his bravery, General Washington asked Congress to promote him. General Washington's opinion of Lafayette continued to grow, and he gave him a command of a division of troops.

Lafayette spent the harsh winter of 1777–1778 with General Washington at Valley Forge. The soldiers suffered from a severe shortage of clothing, food, uniforms, and muskets. Hundreds died from disease. Lafayette used his own money to purchase uniforms and muskets for his men.

Lafayette had become one of the general's most trusted military leaders. In fact, he helped thwart a plot against General Washington. Known as the Conway Cabal, it was an effort by a group of military officers to force Washington to give up command of the Continental Army. They wanted to replace him with General Horatio Gates.

Reproduction of Hand-Colored Lithograph by Currier and Ives
Source: Library of Congress

Although the Conway Cabal did not manage to replace Washington, those involved were successful in achieving another one of their goals—that of getting Lafayette away from Valley Forge. Congress ordered Lafayette to take charge of the newly created Northern Army and to invade Canada. The aim was to win the territory from Britain and to return it to France. Lafayette reluctantly accepted the assignment.

The mission was very difficult, and when less than half of the expected reinforcements arrived in Albany, Lafayette was forced to abort the mission and return to Valley Forge. When he arrived there, he was pleased to learn that the United States and France had signed a Treaty of Alliance,

Think About It

1. Look at the print on the previous page. When and where did Washington and Lafayette meet?

2. How would you describe the mood of the meeting?

3. What can you tell about the people gathered in the print from the way they are dressed?

4. What do the excerpts below from the letter General Washington sent to Lafayette tell us about their relationship?

TRANSCRIPTION OF BEGINNING AND END EXCERPTS OF LETTER FROM

Mount Vernon April 28th–1 May 1788

I have now before me, my dear Marqs your favor of the 3d of August in the last year; together with those of the 1st of January, the 2d of January and the 4th of February in the present—Though the first is of so antient a date, they all came to hand lately, and nearly at the same moment. The frequency of your kind remembrance of me, and the endearing expressions of attachment, are by so much the more satisfactory, as I recognise them to be a counterpart of my own feelings for you. In truth, you know I speak the language of sincerity and not of flattery, when I tell you, that your letters are ever most wellcome and dear to me.

....

Mrs Washington, while she requests that her best Compliments may be presented to you, Joins with me in soliciting that the same friendly and affectionate memorial of our constant remembrance and good wishes may be made acceptable to Madam de la Fayette and the little ones—I am &c.

Go. Washington

John Paul Jones
Naval Hero

Background Information

John Paul—the Jones was added later—was born on July 6, 1747, in the southwestern part of Scotland. He began his sea career at age 13 as apprentice to a merchant on the brig *Friendship*. At age 21 he was given command of a ship, the brig *John*. The *John* made regular runs between British ports and the West Indies.

For several years Paul enjoyed success as a merchant dealing in West Indies trade; however, an incident aboard the *John* caused him to change course. There had been an uprising among the crew, and the seaman disciplined by Paul later died as a result. John Paul was imprisoned for a short time and then let out on bail. Although Paul insisted that he acted in self-defense, the dead man was from an influential Scottish family, and John Paul feared that he would not get a fair trial if he stayed in Scotland. He decided to emigrate to the British colonies in North America. It was at this time that he also decided to add "Jones" to his name.

Painting by Charles Willson Peale

When war broke out in America, John Paul Jones was in Virginia. Sympathetic to the American cause, Jones was eager to fight on the side of the Patriots. Because of his friendship with Joseph Hewes, who was a delegate to the Continental Congress, and his sea-faring experience, in December 1775 Jones was made first lieutenant and second in command of the *Alfred*. When he raised the Grand Union Flag on the *Alfred*, he became the first to hoist an American flag on an American naval vessel.

Before long Jones was given command of the sloop *Providence*. He and his crew were highly successful at capturing British vessels. Jones was rewarded for his accomplishments. When he was transferred back to the *Alfred*, it was as a captain in the Continental Navy.

Early in 1779 the French king gave Captain Jones an old East Indian merchant ship. Jones had it repaired and renamed it the *Bonhomme Richard* in honor of Benjamin Franklin. Franklin's *Poor Richard's Almanac* was published in France under the title *Les Maximes du Bonhomme Richard*. With the *Bonhomme Richard* as the flagship, in August 1779 Jones commanded a fleet of four other ships and two French privateers. His goal was to raid one or more fleets of merchant ships that would be returning to England guarded by British warships.

As he had anticipated, on September 23 the crew spotted a convoy of 41 merchant ships. The ships were being escorted by two British warships, the *Serapis* and the *Countess*. The battle between the *Bonhomme Richard* and the *Serapis* would become one of the most famous battles in the history of the American Navy.

The two warships were locked in battle for hours. Knowing that the *Bonhomme Richard* was in bad shape, Richard Pearson, captain of the *Serapis,* asked Jones if he was ready to surrender. John Paul Jones responded with his now famous reply: "I have not yet begun to fight."

A short time later the Americans exploded a grenade below the decks of the *Serapis*. In spite of the superior power of the British warship and to the surprise of his men, Captain Pearson was forced to surrender. Because the *Bonhomme Richard* was damaged beyond repair, however, Captain Jones ordered the Grand Union Flag to be hoisted on the *Serapis,* and he transferred to that ship.

John Paul Jones tried to convince Congress of the need for a strong navy in order to prevent the nation from future attacks. Congress did not want to spend the money and instead disbanded the Continental Navy. John Paul Jones never got another ship; nevertheless, he will always be remembered as the "Father of the American Navy."

Think About It

1. If you look carefully at the portrait, you will see that Jones is wearing a wearing a medal hanging from a ribbon through his buttonhole. Research and find out what type of medal it was.

2. Read the account by Lieutenant Richard Dale on the following page and then study the painting below. Use your inference skills to determine which battleship is the *Bonhomme Richard* and which is the *Serapis*. Explain.

3. The lieutenant wrote that he "received orders from Commodore Jones to commence de action with a broadside, which indeed appeared to be simultaneous on board both ships." Describe in your own words the action that took place.

4. The two ships were lashed together. Which side tied them together? How do you know?

5. When Jones was asked whether or not his ship had struck, he responded, "I have not yet begun to fight." Use this response to determine the meaning of "struck."

6. When did the *Serapis* surrender?

9. The surrender was a surprise to those on the *Serapis*. How do we know this and why was it a surprise?

Engraving Based on the Painting "Action Between the *Serapis* and *Bonhomme Richard*" by Richard Paton, Published 1780

TRANSCRIPTION OF EXCERPTS FROM ACCOUNT BY LIEUTENANT RICHARD DALE

On the 23d of September, 1779, being below, was roused by an unusual no~se upon deck. This induced me to go upon deck when I found the men were swaying up the royal yards, preparatory to making sail for a large fleet under our lee. I asked the coasting pilot what fleet it was?

He answered, "The Baltic fleet under convoy of the Serapis of 44 guns and the Countess of Scarborough of 20 guns."

....

At about eight, being within hail, the Serapis demanded, "What ship is that? "

He was answered, "I can't hear what you say."

Immediately after, the Serapis hailed again, "What ship is that? Answer immediately, or I shall be under the necessity of firing into you."

At this moment I received orders from Commodore Jones to commence de action with a broadside, which indeed appeared to be simultaneous on board both ships.

....

We had remained in this situation but a few minutes when we were again hailed by the Serapis, "Has your ship struck?"

To which Captain Jones answered, "I have not yet begun to fight!"

As we were unable to bring a single gun to bear upon the Serapis our topsails were backed, while those of the Serapis being filled, the ships separated. The Serapis bore short round upon her heel, and her jibboom ran into the mizen rigging of the Bon Homme Richard In this situation the ships were made fast together with a hawser, the bowsprit of the Serapis to the mizen- I mast of the Bon Homme Richard, and the action recommenced from the star- I board sides of the two ships. With a view of separating the ships, the Serapis I let go her anchor, which manoeuver brought her head and the stern of the Bon Homme Richard to the wind, while the ships lay closely pressed against each other.

A novelty in naval combats was now presented to many witnesses, but to few admirers. The rammers were run into the respective ships to enable the men to load after the lower ports of the Serapis had been blown away, to make room for running out their guns, and in this situation the ships remained until between 10 and 11 o'clock P.M., when the engagement terminated by the surrender of the Serapis.

From the commencement to the termination of the action there was not a man on board the Bon Homme Richard ignorant of the superiority of the Serapis, both in weight of metal and in the qualities of the crews both in weight of metal and in the qualities of the crews. The crew of that ship was picked seamen, and the ship itself had been only a few months off the stocks, whereas the crew of the Bon Homme Richard consisted of part Americans, English and French, and a part of Maltese, Portuguese and Malays, these latter contributing by their want of naval skill and knowledge of the English language to depress rather than to elevate a just hope of success in a combat under such circumstances.

....

Upon finding that the flag of the Serapis had been struck, I went to Captain Jones and asked whether I might board the Serapis, to which he consented...and- jumping upon the gun-wale, seized the main-brace pennant and swung m~self upon her quarter-deck.

....

I found Captain Pearson standing on the leeward side of the quarter-deck and, addressing myself to him, said, "Sir, I have orders to send you on board the ship alongside." The first lieutenant of the Serapis coming up at this moment inquired of Captain Pearson whether the ship alongside had struck to him, To which I replied, "No, Sir, the contrary: he has struck to us."

The lieutenant renewed his inquiry, "Have you struck, Sir?"

"Yes, I have."

....

Paying for the War
Robert Morris

Background Information

At the start of the revolution the odds of the American colonies defeating Great Britain in an eight-year war were not good. Britain had many advantages. It was a wealthy empire with the ability to tax its subjects. Its excellent credit rating enabled it to borrow money if needed.

For the Americans, on the other hand, paying for the war would be a daunting task. They did what they could:

1. The individual states issued their own currency; however, the currency had little value.

2. Some states seized and sold property owned by Loyalists.

3. The Continental Congress printed money. Although it seemed to represent specie, however, there was no actual gold, silver, or other precious metal backing the money. Therefore, the paper currency had no real value. To make matters worse, counterfeiters printed money and widely distributed it. It is no wonder the saying "Not worth a Continental" spread.

Engraving by Ole Erekson, c. 1876

4. The Continental Congress tried to obtain loans from other countries.

By 1781 Congress was facing a real crisis and created a new position, Secretary of Finance. It appointed Congressman Robert Morris to that office. Morris was a wealthy merchant from Philadelphia with an interest in a successful shipping company. He had originally been against declaring independence from Britain because he did not think the colonists had a chance to win. Once the move was made, however, he did all he could to support the war cause.

Upon his appointment as Secretary of Finance, Morris took immediate emergency measures. One of the first things he did was to devalue the dollar. He also got the states to give Congress about $2,000,000 in specie to back the currency. Another, more controversial action was to pay the Continental Army in debt certificates, deferring actual pay until after the war.

In 1781 Robert Morris submitted a plan to Congress for the establishment of a national bank. His proposal was approved, and the Bank of North America was created. This was an important step towards building up the credit of the United States with European nations. It was done with the authority given to Congress by the Articles of Confederation, which was ratified on March 1, 1781. In order to ensure success, Congress appointed Morris Superintendent of Finance of the United States.

Robert Morris's work as Secretary of Finance was important, but he did much more than that. Morris negotiated loans from France and other nations. He got states to provide supplies and he made sure those supplies reached the troops. He was responsible for most of the gunpowder given to the troops. What's more, he used his personal funds and credit to finance the war effort.

Without Morris the outcome of the war might have been different. Washington appreciated his contributions and when he became President, he offered Robert Morris the position of the nation's first Secretary of the Treasury. Morris declined and suggested that he appoint Alexander Hamilton instead.

Etching: "A Picturesque View of the State of the Nation for February 1778"
Illustration from *Westminster Magazine*, v. 6 (1778 Mar. 1)
Source: Library of Congress

Scene from "The Apotheosis of Washington," a
Fresco above the Rotunda of the U.S. Capitol Building, by Brumidi

© **Barbara M. Peller**   *Using Primary Sources to Teach U.S. History: War to Constitution*   47

Think About It

1. Use context clues to help you explain the meaning of "specie" in the Background.

2. Analyze the "Picturesque View of the State of the Nation for February 1778." Explain what each of the following symbolizes: the man with a feathered cap cutting the horns off a cow, the cow, the person milking the cow, and the two men holding bowls of milk.

3. In that same etching, what do you think the lion and dog represent?

4. What is the purpose of this scene from "The Apotheosis of Washington"?

5. In this scene, Robert Morris is receiving something. What is it and who is giving it to him? How do you know?

6. This scene is called "Commerce." What did the artist include to reinforce this theme?

7. Use clues from the visual to infer what the next scene in the fresco represents.

8. Define "apotheosis" and evaluate the title.

Paying for the War
Haym Salomon

Background Information

Haym Salomon was a Polish-born Jewish immigrant. By the time of the American Revolution, he had become a highly successful financial broker. He used his success to help finance the war at great sacrifice to himself and his family.

Robert Morris and Haym Salomon often worked together to provide support to the war effort. In fact, the two men carried out more than seventy-five financial transactions between 1781 and 1784.

Salomon acted as broker for the sale of bonds to pay war expenses and the salaries of government officials. He was also a major broker for subsidies from France, Spain, and Holland. In addition, he was authorized to sell merchandise that was seized by privateers who were on the Patriots' side. Salomon even contributed the commissions he made on these transactions.

Haym Salomon, Unknown Origin

Salomon's reputation spread. In August 1781 General Washington's troops were in dire need of food, uniforms, and other supplies. Realizing that the men were bordering on mutiny, he told Robert Morris that he needed $20,000 for the campaign he was about to conduct at Yorktown. When Morris informed him that there were neither funds nor credit, Washington ordered him, "Send for Haym Salomon."

Salomon raised the money for Washington's campaign by selling bills of exchange, types of promissory notes. He also gave Robert Morris a large personal loan. General Washington was able to conduct the Yorktown campaign as planned. It turned out to be the last land battle of the American Revolution.

Throughout the war, Haym Salomon gave a large sum of his own money to the government. Promissory notes and other evidence show that he advanced more than $658,000—a huge sum at that time—to help the war effort. Sadly, when he died suddenly at only forty-five years of age, he was bankrupt. He never received payment for his loans. Neither did his wife nor four children.

Think About It

1. To what cause does this commemorative stamp refer? How did Haym Salomon contribute to that cause?

2. Research and find out who the other three people in this series were. Describe their contributions to the cause.

3. Do you agree that Salomon was a hero? Give reasons.

Siege of Yorktown
Lord Cornwallis Surrenders

Background Information

In August 1781 General Charles Cornwallis and his men marched into Virginia. They seized Yorktown and Gloucester, located on each side of the York River. General Cornwallis and his troops settled in Yorktown.

General Washington was near New York and had been planning to attack the city with the help of French troops under the command of the Comte de Rochambeau. However, when he learned that a large fleet from the French West Indies, led by the French admiral De Grasse, was in New York and on its way to Virginia, Washington changed his strategy. He decided instead to attempt to defeat Cornwallis at Yorktown.

Washington knew that the Marquis de Lafayette was in Virginia with an American army. He ordered them to go to Yorktown and to prevent General Cornwallis and his men from leaving Yorktown by land.

Portrait of Cornwallis
by John Singleton Copley

Meanwhile, Rochambeau, Washington, and their troops met in New York. With the assistance of de Grasse's fleet, the troops crossed the Hudson River. They then began their long march to Virginia, reaching the Chesapeake Bay in mid-September. Again with the help of the fleet led by the Comte de Grasse, the American and French troops sailed down the Chesapeake to Yorktown.

De Grasee then set out to defeat the British fleet in the Battle of the Chesapeake. His success prevented the British from sending reinforcements to Cornwallis. De Grasse's fleet then blockaded the coast. At the same time, Washington and Rochambeau met Lafayette as planned. General Washington's plan to encircle Cornwallis at Yorktown was complete.

General Cornwallis knew he was outnumbered. His 9,000 British and Hessian soldiers were no match for the 17,000 American and French troops. For three weeks Washington's men bombarded Cornwallis's men. Cornwallis hoped for reinforcements, but they would not arrive in time to help.

The British suffered great losses—not just from the attack but also from disease and the lack of supplies. Cornwallis attempted to evacuate his troops, but bad weather kept him from carrying out that plan. Finally, on October 17, 1781, General Cornwallis raised a flag of truce.

Portrait of Washington
By Charles Peale Polk

The terms of the surrender were written in the Articles of Capitulation, which was signed by Cornwallis on October 19. At two o'clock, when the formal surrender was to take place, Cornwallis did not attend. Claiming he was ill, he sent Brigadier General Charles O'Hara, his second in command, to surrender his sword. Washington, refusing to accept the sword of anyone but Cornwallis, appointed General Benjamin Lincoln to accept it.

Although it is not certain, many accounts say that as the British army marched off the field, their band played "The World Turned Upside Down."

The Battle of Yorktown was the last major land battle of the war. Peace talks would begin in September 1782, and on September 3, 1783, the Treaty of Paris would formally recognize the United States as a free and independent nation.

Articles of Capitulation, settled between his Excellency General Washington, Commander in Chief of the combined forces of America and France; His Excellency the Count de Rochambeau, Lieutenant General of the armies of the King of France, Great Cross of the royal and military order of St. Louis, commanding the auxiliary troops of His Most Christian Majesty in America; and His Excellency, the Count de Grasse, Lieutenant General of the naval armies of His Most Christian Majesty, Commander of the order of St. Louis, commanding in chief the naval army of France in the Chesapeak — on the one part. — And the Right Honorable Earl Cornwallis, Lieutenant General of His Britannic Majesty's forces, commanding the garrisons of York and Gloucester; and Thomas Symonds Esquire commanding His Britannic Majesty's naval forces in York River, in Virginia — on the other part.

Article 1.

The garrisons of York and Gloucester, including the officers and seamen of His Britannic Majesty's ships, as well as other mariners, to surrender themselves prisoners of war to the combined forces of America and France. The land troops to remain prisoners to the United States — the navy to the naval army of His Most Christian Majesty.

Article 1.

Granted.

This is the first page of the Articles of Capitulation, which listed the terms of the surrender. This copy was drafted by Samuel Shaw, Henry Knox's aide-de-camp. Knox had been instrumental in the victory at Yorktown.

TRANSCRIPTION

Articles of Capitulation, Yorktown

Settled between his Excellency General Washington, Commander-in-Chief of the combined Forces of America and France; his Excellency the Count de Rochambeau, Lieutenant-General of the Armies of the King of France, Great Cross of the royal and military Order of St. Louis, commanding the auxiliary Troops of his Most Christian Majesty in America; and his Excellency the Count de Grasse, Lieutenant-General of the Naval Armies of his Most Christian Majesty, Commander of the Order of St. Louis, Commander-in-Chief of the Naval Army of France in the Chesapeake, on the one Part; and the Right Honorable Earl Cornwallis, Lieutenant-General of his Britannic Majesty's Forces, commanding the Garrisons of York and Gloucester; and Thomas Symonds, Esquire, commanding his Britannic Majesty's Naval Forces in York River in Virginia, on the other Part.

Article I. The garrisons of York and Gloucester including the officers and seamen of his Britannic Majesty's ships, as well as other mariners, to surrender themselves prisoners of war to the combined forces of America and France. The land troops to remain prisoners to the United States, the navy to the naval army of his Most Christian Majesty.

Article II. The artillery, arms, accoutrements, military chest, and public stores of every denomination, shall be delivered unimpaired to the heads of departments appointed to receive them.

Article III. At twelve o'clock this day the two redoubts on the left flank of York to be delivered, the one to a detachment of American infantry, the other to a detachment of French grenadiers.

The garrison of York will march out to a place to be appointed in front of the posts, at two o'clock precisely, with shouldered arms, colors cased, and drums beating a British or German march. They are then to ground their arms, and return to their encampments, where they will remain until they are despatched to the places of their destination. Two works on the Gloucester side will be delivered at one o'clock to a detachment of French and American troops appointed to possess them. The garrison will march out at three o'clock in the afternoon; the cavalry with their swords drawn, trumpets sounding, and the infantry in the manner prescribed for the garrison of York. They are likewise to return to their encampments until they can be finally marched off.

Article IV. Officers are to retain their side-arms. Both officers and soldiers to keep their private property of every kind; and no part of their baggage or papers to be at any time subject to search or inspection. The baggage and papers of officers and soldiers taken during the siege to be likewise preserved for them. It is understood that any property obviously belonging to the inhabitants of these States, in the possession of the garrison, shall be subject to be reclaimed.

Article V. The soldiers to be kept in Virginia, Maryland, or Pennsylvania, and as much by regiments as possible, and supplied with the same rations of provisions as are allowed to soldiers in the service of America. A field-officer from each nation, to wit, British, Anspach, and Hessian, and other officers on parole, in the proportion of one to fifty men to be allowed to reside near their respective regiments, to visit them frequently, and be witnesses of their treatment; and that their officers may receive and deliver clothing and other necessaries for them, for which passports are to be granted when applied for.

Article VI. The general, staff, and other officers not employed as mentioned in the above articles, and who choose it, to be permitted to go on parole to Europe, to New York, or to any other American maritime posts at present in the possession of the British forces, at their own option; and proper vessels to be granted by the Count de Grasse to carry them under flags of truce to New York within ten days from this date, if possible, and they to reside in a district to be agreed upon hereafter, until they embark. The officers of the civil department of the army and navy to be included in this article. Passports to go by land to be granted to those to whom vessels cannot be furnished.

Article VII. Officers to be allowed to keep soldiers as servants, according to the common practice of the service. Servants not soldiers are not to be considered as prisoners, and are to be allowed to attend their masters.

Article VIII. The Bonetta sloop-of-war to be equipped, and navigated by its present captain and crew, and left entirely at the disposal of Lord Cornwallis from the hour that the capitulation is signed, to receive an aid-de-camp to carry despatches to Sir Henry Clinton; and such soldiers as he may think proper to send to New York, to be permitted to sail without examination.

When his despatches are ready, his Lordship engages on his part, that the ship shall be delivered to the order of the Count de Grasse, if she escapes the dangers of the sea. That she shall not carry off any public stores. Any part of the crew that may be deficient on her return, and the soldiers passengers, to be accounted for on her delivery.

Article IX. The traders are to preserve their property, and to be allowed three months to dispose of or remove them; and those traders are not to be considered as prisoners of war. The traders will be allowed to dispose of their effects, the allied army having the right of preemption. The traders to be considered as prisoners of war upon parole.

Article X. Natives or inhabitants of different parts of this country, at present in York or Gloucester, are not to be punished on account of having joined the British army. This article cannot be assented to, being altogether of civil resort.

Article XI. Proper hospitals to be furnished for the sick and wounded. They are to be attended by their own surgeons on parole; and they are to be furnished with medicines and stores from the American hospitals. The hospital stores now at York and Gloucester shall be delivered for the use of the British sick and wounded. Passports will be granted for procuring them further supplies from New York, as occasion may require; and proper hospitals will be furnished for the reception of the sick and wounded of the two garrisons.

Article XII. Wagons to be furnished to carry the baggage of the officers attending the soldiers, and to surgeons when traveling on account of the sick, attending the hospitals at public expense. They are to be furnished if possible.

Article XIII. The shipping and boats in the two harbours, with all their stores, guns, tackling, and apparel, shall be delivered up in their present state to an officer of the navy appointed to take possession of them, previously unloading the private property, part of which had been on board for security during the siege.

Article XIV. No article of capitulation to be infringed on pretence of reprisals; and if there be any doubtful expressions in it, they are to be interpreted according to the common meaning and acceptation of the words.

Done at Yorktown, in Virginia, October 19th, 1781.
Cornwallis, Thomas Symonds.
Done in the Trenches before Yorktown, in Virginia, October 19th, 1781.
George Washington,
Le Comte de Rochambeau,
Le Comte de Barras, En mon nom & celui du Comte de Grasse.

Think About It: Articles of Capitulation

1. Which article describes how the troops will surrender? Describe how they should surrender and what they should do after surrendering their arms.

2. Article XIII caused some controversy. What was the cause of the controversy?

3. With what topic did article XI deal?

© Barbara M. Peller

Think About It: Lithograph

1. Do you think this lithograph correctly depicted the event? Does it give a good idea of the event? Explain.

2. Compare the demeanor of the Americans with that of the British soldiers.

3. Evaluate General Cornwallis's decision not to attend the ceremony.

4. What do the ships along the coast and the men and flag at the top of the hill suggest?

Surrender of Cornwallis, Copy of Lithograph by James S. Baillie, 1845
Source: National Archives

The Articles of Confederation
America's First Constitution

Background Information

The Articles of Confederation was the first written constitution of the United States of America. It provided that the new nation would be a confederacy, a form of government in which the states are joined mainly for defense. The individual states would remain independent in most other regards.

Several drafts were presented to the committee in charge of drafting the document. The one that finally was submitted to the Continental Congress for consideration in November 1777 was written mostly by John Dickerson. Congress discussed many issues before voting on the final document. In order for the document to go into effect, it would have to be approved by all thirteen states. During the debates, the delegates were basically divided into two groups: the Radicals and the Conservatives.

The Radicals believed that the purpose of the revolution was the formation of a government in the form of a confederation. They also thought that most of the power should be in the hands of the states and that the main function of the confederation should be national defense.

The Conservatives believed that the war had been fought to eliminate the control of a foreign power and to give control to a new, strong central government. They, too, thought that the central government should be responsible for the mutual defense of the states; however, they wanted to extend the central government's powers to other areas as well.

By 1779 twelve states had ratified it; only Maryland refused to accept it. Maryland would not approve it because several states had made claims to western lands. Like the other states that could not expand westward, Maryland held the view that the western lands belonged to the United States and not to the individual states. Maryland feared that if Virginia's claims were approved, that state would totally dominate it.

When Thomas Jefferson finally convinced Virginia to set aside its claims with the provision that the territory would be divided into new states, Maryland ratified the document. The Articles of Confederation went into effect on March 1, 1781.

In the final document, the new government was to be a confederation that served as a "league of friendship" formed with the intent of defending one another. Each state maintained its sovereignty and was said to hold any right to govern that was not specifically given to the national government.

These were some of the express powers given to the Confederation Congress:
- the power to deal with foreign nations, including the power to declare war or make peace;
- the power to deal with Native Americans;
- the ability to regulate the army and navy;
- the duty to run the post office;
- the right to try crimes committed on the high seas; and
- as a last resort, the power to resolve disputes that arise between the states.

The Articles further stated that in matters of foreign affairs, nine states must agree. It also included a provision that any change to the Articles must be approved by all thirteen states.

The Articles of Confederation was not a perfect document, but it did mark the commitment of the states to join together as a permanent union called the United States of America.

© Barbara M. Peller

Page One of the Articles of Confederation

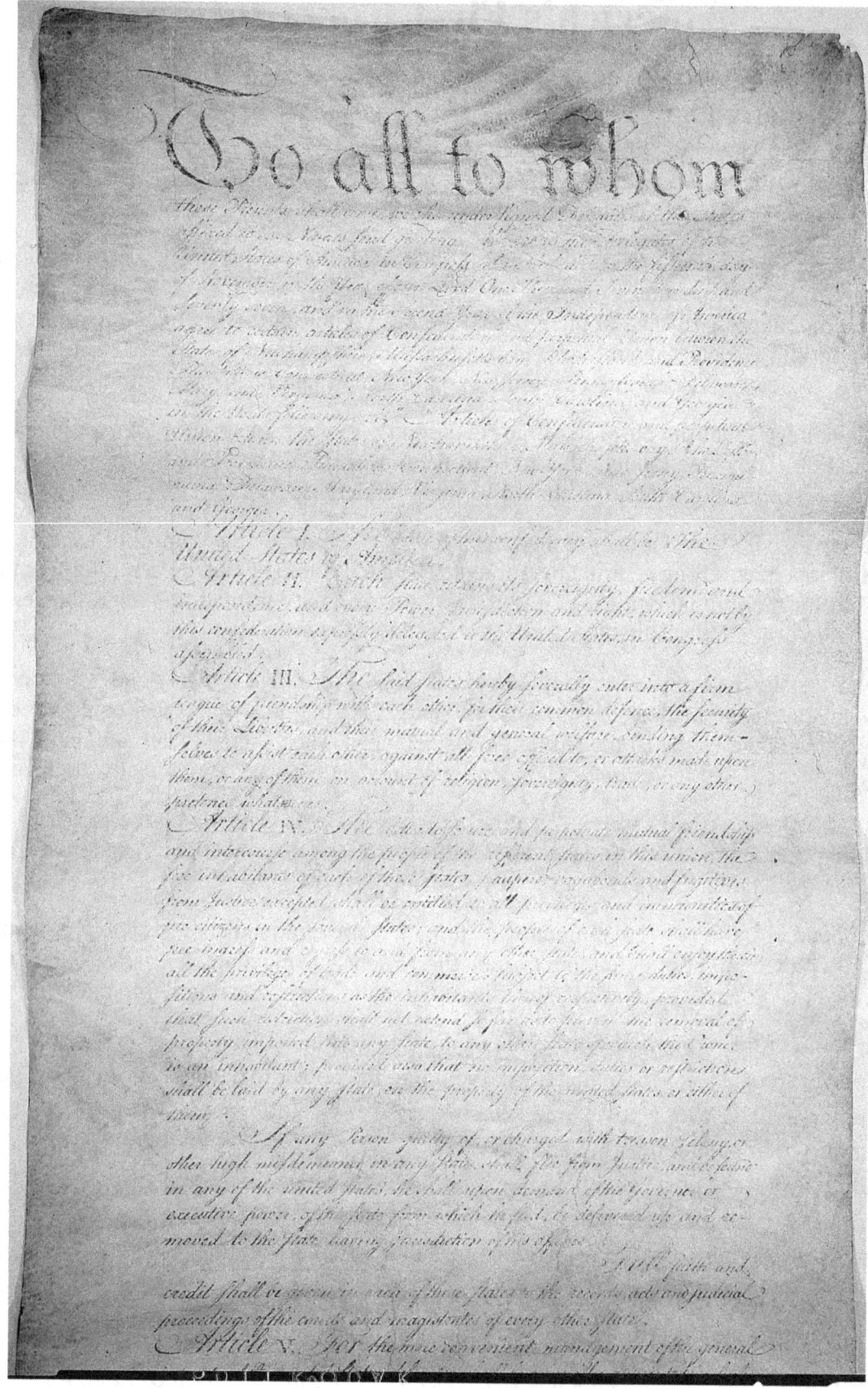

Page One of the Articles of Confederation
(No Higher Resolution of the Original Document Is Available)

TRANSCRIPTION OF THE TITLE AND FIRST FOUR ARTICLES OF THE ARTICLES OF CONFEDERATION

Articles of confederation and perpetual union between the states of New Hampshire, Massachusetts Bay, Rhode Island, and Providence plantations, Connecticut, New York, New Jersey, Pennsylvania, Delaware, Maryland, Virginia, North Carolina, South Carolina, and Georgia

Article I. The style of this confederacy shall be "The UNITED STATES of AMERICA.

Art. II. Each state retains its sovereignty, freedom, and independence, and every power, jurisdiction, and right, which is not by this confederation expressly delegated to the United States, in Congress assembled.

Art. III. The said states hereby severally enter into a firm league of friendship with each other for their common defence, the security of their liberties, and their mutual and general welfare, binding themselves to assist each other against all force offered to or attacks made upon them, or any of them, on account of religion, sovereignty, trade, or any other pretence whatever.

Art. IV. The better to secure and perpetuate mutual friendship and Intercourse among the people of the different states in this union, the free inhabitants of each of these states, (paupers, vagabonds, and fugitives from justice, excepted) shall be entitled to all privileges and immunities of free citizens in the several states; and the people of each state shall have free ingress and regress to and from any other state, and shall enjoy therein all the privileges of trade and commerce, subject to the same duties, impositions, and restrictions, as the inhabitants thereof respectively. Provided that such restriction shall not extend so far as to prevent the removal of property imported into any state to any other state of which the owner is an inhabitant; provided also, that no imposition, duties, or restriction, shall be laid by any state on the property of the United States, or either of them.

NOTE: A transcription of the complete Articles of Confederation can be found in the Appendix.

Think About It

1. From reading the first four articles of the document, judge who had more influence on the creation of the Articles of Confederation: the Radicals or the Conservatives. Give reasons for your opinion.

2. Only one branch of government was provided for in the Articles of Confederation. Which branch was created? In your opinion, why was this a problem?

Treaty of Paris of 1783
An Official End to the American Revolution!

Background Information

Peace talks began in April 1782 following the victory of the American and French forces at Yorktown, Virginia. Although the Americans negotiated a separate agreement with Great Britain, the war had really been an international conflict also involving France, Spain, and Holland, which had provided aid to the Americans. They, too, signed agreements with Great Britain now that the fighting had ended.

The Continental Congress appointed a committee of five members to begin the negotiation with Britain. The nations agreed that the location of the negotiation would be Paris, France. John Adams, Benjamin Franklin, and John Jay went to Paris. The two other members, Thomas Jefferson and Henry Laurens, did not. Harsh winter weather caused Jefferson to delay his travel plans too long to enable him to attend. Henry Laurens was captured by a British warship and was held in the tower of London until the end of the war. Laurens arrived in Paris two days before the preliminary articles of peace were signed on November 30, 1782.

About ten months later the final treaty—the Treaty of Paris of 1783—was signed. In addition to officially ending the war between the United States and Great Britain, it had many important provisions. The following were among the most significant:

1. Great Britain recognized the independence of the United States from Great Britain. Great Britain would treat all thirteen states as free, sovereign states.

2. The agreement established the borders of the United States. Great Britain relinquished all the land it held from the Allegheny Mountains on the east and the Mississippi River on the west. The result was that the territory of the United States basically doubled in size.

3. Although there were some limitations, important fishing rights involving Canadian waters were given to American fishermen.

4. The Americans would not treat the Loyalists who remained in America with cruelty. Also, property confiscated from the Loyalists would be returned to them.

The Treaty of Paris. which formally ended the war, was signed on September 3, 1783. The Continental Congress, which was temporarily located in Annapolis, Maryland, at the time, ratified the agreement on January 14, 1784.

The agreement left several border regions unclear or in dispute. Those issues would be dealt with in future agreements in the years to come. Although the treaty was not perfect, on a whole, it was most beneficial for the United States. Most importantly, it was firmly established as a sovereign, independent nation free of control by any foreign entity.

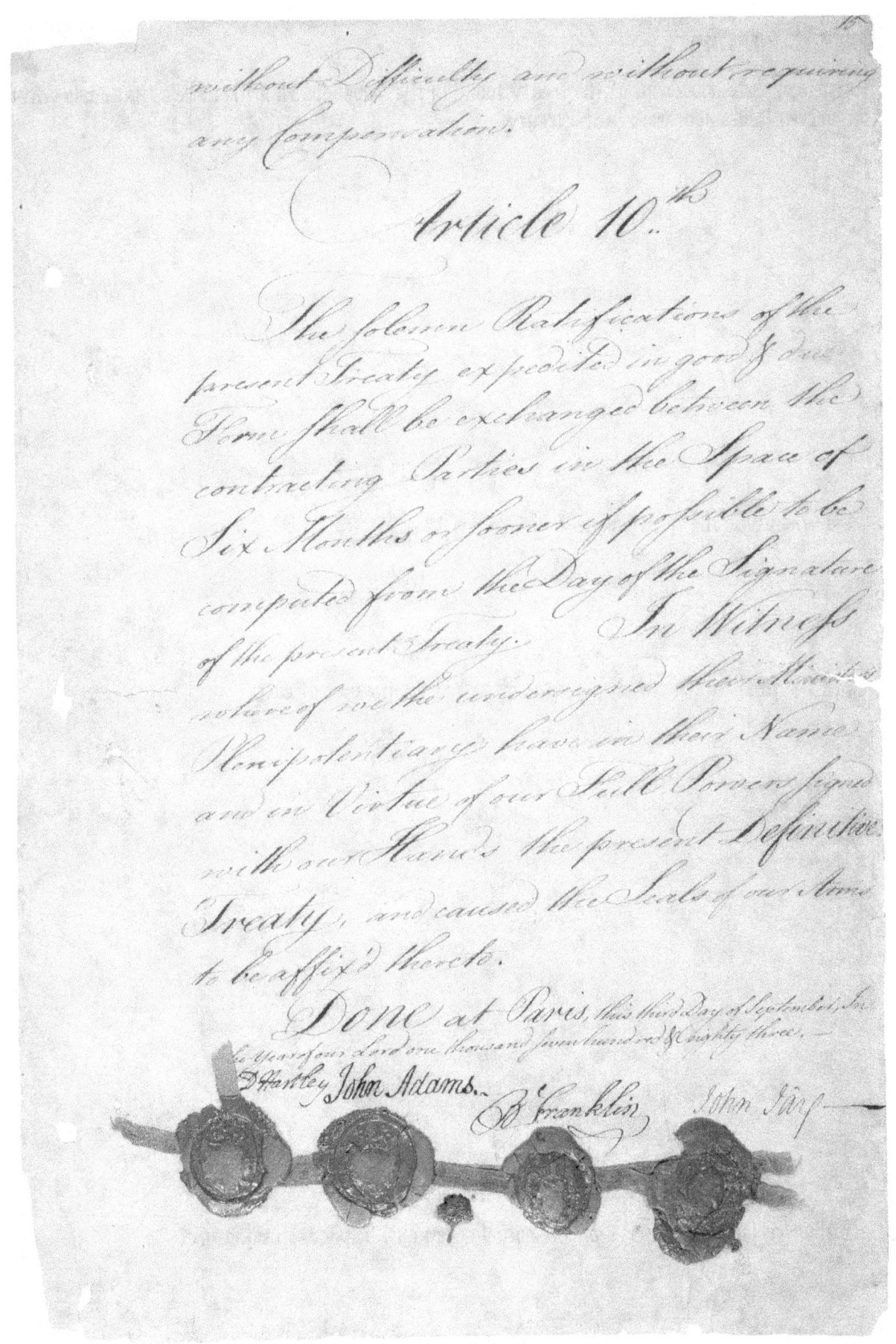

Treaty of Paris of 1783
Last Page of Final Document

Think About It: Document

1. Refer to the complete transcript of the treaty found in the Appendix. Find the article that deals with each of the four important issues addressed in the treaty.

2. Where and when was the treaty signed?

3. Who signed the final agreement? Explain the historical significance of each.

4. What are the circular marks (in red on the actual document) below each signature?

Benjamin West, *The American Peace Commissioners*

Benjamin West's painting was meant to be portray the commissioners who were negotiating the agreement between the United States and Great Britain in Paris. From left to right the men in the painting are John Jay, John Adams, Benjamin Franklin, Henry Laurens, and William Temple Franklin, all of whom represented the United States in the negotiation.

Think About It: Painting

1. This painting was left unfinished. Can you figure out why?

2. If you were the artist, would you have finished it? How might you have accomplished this?

The American Peace Commissioners, by Benjamin West

Shays' Rebellion
The Articles of Confederation Are Put to the Test

Background Information

Daniel Shays was a farm laborer. He joined the Massachusetts militia early in the revolutionary war and fought in that war for five years, rising to the rank of captain. Probably because he was wounded in battle, he never received pay for his military service.

When he returned to his home in Brookfield, a town in rural western Massachusetts, Shays was dismayed to learn that he was being taken to court for unpaid debts that had piled up while he was fighting in the war. Because he had not been paid for his service, he was unable to pay those debts.

Shays soon learned that he was not alone. High taxes had put many farmers in his part of the state in danger of going bankrupt and losing their farm. The Massachusetts legislature, backed by the eastern merchants and bankers, would not take steps to help those in economic crisis. Steps that other states had taken included passing laws to forgive debt, allowing payment of debts to be made in the form of crops, and printing more paper money. Instead, local sheriffs seized many farms and imprisoned those who could not pay their debts.

Many rallied around Shays, who by 1786 had become a leader in the resistance. Although it started with peaceful petitions, the rebellion soon escalated. The rebels carried out several actions that angered Governor Bowdoin. They confiscated seized property and returned it to their owners. They prevented the county court in Northampton from opening. They shut down the court in Worcester.

Governor Bowdoin was intent upon putting an end to the rebellion. Because the Massachusetts militia was sympathetic to the protesters, he organized a private militia. Bankers and merchants from the eastern part of the state helped fund the private military force.

In January 1787 Shays and about 1,200 followers, sometimes called Shaysites, marched to the federal gun arsenal in Springfield. They were met by the strong army that Bowdoin had recruited. The skirmish that followed resulted in the death of four protesters and the wounding of twenty. It also led to the imprisonment of about 150 protesters, some of whom where sentenced to death.

Shays managed to flee to Vermont, where he remained until the protesters, including him, were pardoned. He returned to Massachusets. Eventually, he was even given the pay due to him for his five years of military service during the war.

Although Governor Bowdoin managed to put down the rebellion, Shays Rebellion was proof to many that the Articles of Confederation were inadequate to meet the needs of the nation. The Constitutional Convention in Philadelphia met between May and September of 1787 to address the problems of the weak central government. Shays Rebellion and similar occurrences caused George Washington, Alexander Hamilton, James Madison, and others to rethink the adequacy of the Articles and to urge support for the Constitution.

"Shays's Rebellion." The portraits of Daniel Shays and Job Shattuck, leaders of the Massachusetts "Regulators,"
Cover of Bickerstaff's *Boston Almanack* of 1787

Think About It
Cover of Bickerstaff's *Boston Almanack*

1. This copy of a contemporary engraving depicts the artist's conception of Daniel Shays (left) and Job Shattuck, another rebel leader. The artist probably never met either one. How might the way in which he drew them give us insight into whether or not the artist was sympathetic to their cause?

2. Analyze the portraits of the two rebels and explain what each of these elements represents: the swords, the uniforms, the flag, and the cannon.

Excerpts of Letters Written by George Washington Regarding Shays' Rebellion

To Henry Lee, October 31, 1786
"The accounts which are published of the commotions. . . exhibit a melancholy proof of what our trans-Atlantic foe has predicted; and of another thing perhaps, which is still more to be regretted, and is yet more unaccountable, **that mankind when left to themselves are unfit for their own Government. I am mortified beyond expression** when I view the clouds that have spread over the brightest morn that ever dawned upon any Country. . . **To be more exposed in the eyes of the world, and more contemptible than we already are, is hardly possible.**
Source: The George Washington Papers at the Library of Congress, 1741–1799.

To David Humphreys, October 22, 1786
"Commotions of this sort, like snow-balls, gather strength as they roll, if there is no opposition in the way to divide and crumble them. . . **I am mortified beyond expression that in the moment of our acknowledged independence we should by our conduct verify the predictions of our transatlantic foe,** and render ourselves ridiculous and contemptible in the eyes of all Europe."
Source: The George Washington Papers at the Library of Congress, 1741–1799.

To Henry Knox, February 3, 1787
"The moment is, indeed, important!—**If government shrinks, or is unable to enforce its laws; fresh maneuvers will be displayed by the insurgents—anarchy & confusion must prevail—and every thing will be turned topsy turvey in that State; where it is not probable the mischiefs will terminate.**"
"if three years ago any person had told me that at this day, I should see such a formidable rebellion against the laws & constitutions of our own making as now appears I should have thought him a bedlamite— a fit subject for a mad house."temptible in the eyes of all Europe."
Source: The National Archives

Excerpts of Letters Written by Thomas Jefferson Regarding Shays' Rebellion

To William S. Smith, Paris, Nov. 13, 1787
What country can preserve its liberties if their rulers are not warned from time to time that their people preserve the spirit of resistance? **Let them take arms. . . the tree of liberty must be refreshed from time to time with the blood of patriots** & tyrants.
Source: Library of Congress

To James Madison, Paris, Jan. 30, 1787
I am impatient to learn your sentiments on the late troubles in the Eastern states... I hold it that **a little rebellion now and then is a good thing, & as necessary in the political world as storms in the physical.** . . It is a medicine necessary for the sound health of government.
Source: Library of Congress

To James Madison, Paris, Dec. 20, 1787
The late rebellion in Massachusetts has given more alarm than I think it should have done. Calculate that one rebellion in 13 states in the course of 11 years, is but one for each state in a century & a half. No country should be so long without one. **Nor will any degree of power in the hands of government prevent insurrections.** France, with all its despotism , and two or three hundred thousand men always in arms has had three insurrections in the three years I have been here in every one of which greater numbers were engaged than in Massachusetts & a great deal more blood was spilt.
Source: Library of Congress

To Abigail Adams, Paris, Feb. 22, 1787
The spirit of resistance to government is so valuable on certain occasions, that I wish it to be always kept alive. It **will often be exercised when wrong, but better so than not to be exercised at all.** I like a little rebellion now and then. It is like a storm in the Atmosphere.
Source: Library of Congress

Think About It

1. Read the excerpts on the previous page, paying special attention to the sections in bold. Use the information in them to determine Washington's and Jefferson's points of view regarding Shays' Rebellion.

2. Compare and contrast Washington's and Jefferson's points of view.

The United States Constitution
The Supreme Law of the Land

Background Information

On September 11, 1786, twelve delegates from five states met in Annapolis, Maryland, at the suggestion of James Madison. The given reason was to discuss interstate trade. On September 14, however, Alexander Hamilton introduced a resolution calling for the convening of another convention—this time to discuss the defects of the Articles of Confederation and to amend the articles.

The Constitutional Convention was to be held in New York from May to September 1787. James Madison was the first to arrive, followed by the rest of the Virginia delegation. The meeting officially opened on May 25, when there were enough people to form a quorum. Although the resolution was to revise the Articles of Confederation, many of the delegates proposed the need for a completely new document. Among those in favor were Alexander Hamilton and James Madison.

The first order of business was to choose a president of the convention. George Washington was unanimously elected. William Jackson was elected secretary; however his note-taking was sketchy and not very useful in their deliberations. James Madison, on the other hand, took copious, detailed notes. The delegates often relied upon them when discussing the various issues.

Madison actually worked hard even before the convention officially began. He presented a rough draft containing his ideas to the other members. This draft became known as the Virginia Plan. The delegates agreed to some of the less controversial provisions without much debate. These included the need for a bicameral congress, comprising an upper and a lower house; a separate executive branch; and a separate judicial branch. The delegates would debate the other issues more extensively.

One of the main sources of disagreement was between the large and small states regarding representation. The Virginia Plan called for representation in the lower house to be based upon population. It also called for those representatives to then elect members of the upper house. Small states feared they would have little influence. Some believed this plan would make the federal government too strong.

The New Jersey Plan, introduced by William Paterson, called for equal representation no matter what the size of the state. The small states liked that they remained strong; however, the plan failed to provide for direct representation of the people.

The Connecticut Compromise, also known as the Great Compromise, was proposed to settle the issue of proportional representation. The number of delegates given to each state would be based upon the relative size of the state's population. However, every state would be granted the same number of representatives in the upper house.

The compromise also dealt with some of the conflict regarding slavery. The northern states did not want slaves to be counted because it would give them a population advantage in the lower house. The southern states wanted slaves counted for population assessment but did not want them taxed. The Connecticut Compromise proposed that slaves would be counted as three-fifths of a person for assessment purposes. The compromise was eventually adopted by a slim margin.

Another issue was whether the executive should be one man or three. Some delegates feared having only one man in charge of the executive branch. However, those in favor of having only one man won. The reason was probably because the delegates were fairly certain that George Washington would be elected as the first President of the United States. Issues regarding *how* the executive branch should be elected were not as easy to solve. Madison held the unpopular view that the legislature should elect him. Some thought the governors should do it. In the end it was decided that an electoral college would vote and that if there was no majority, then the states would vote in blocs.

Once the major issues had been fully debated, another committee, the Committee of Detail, was selected to craft the first draft of the Constitution. It would be chaired by John Rutledge. The committee was instructed to create a draft that reflected the agreements arrived at during the debates.

Before the Convention adjourned on July 26, Charles Pinckney of South Carolina and other southerners warned that they would not sign unless more was done to protect the rights of the southern states. They were against regulations that would curtail their slave trade.

The committee returned on August 6. Most of the revisions they made were accepted without much disagreement. However, the committee had made some changes in language in order to appease the southern states. Those changes had these results:

- Congress would not be able to interfere with the slave trade;
- taxation on exports was prohibited; and
- legislation regarding tariffs or quotas on foreign commerce would require a 2/3 majority vote in each house.

The revisions angered the northern states and those who opposed slavery. They wanted Congress to regulate foreign trade. Also, because manufacturing was becoming important in the North, they wanted Congress to impose import duties on goods and raw materials from foreign nations. Eventually a compromise was reached. Congress would have the authority to regulate trade, but it was prohibited from limiting the slave trade for twenty years. Also there would be no export tax.

Most of the revisions made by the committee were accepted and much of what was in the draft became part of the final United States Constitution. Once all of the details were worked out, the document was given to the Committee of [Stile] and Arrangement. It was their responsibility to make sure that the final document included everything agreed to by the delegates. Gouverneur Morris headed the committee and is credited with writing the Preamble as well as the final draft of the Articles themselves.

The final meeting of the Constitutional Convention was held on September 17, 1787, but the work was not over. Forty-one of the 55 original delegates were present. All but 3 of them signed the document. George Mason and Edmund Randolph of Virginia and Elbridge Gerry of Massachusetts did not sign.

Nine states were required to ratify the document in order for it to become the law of the land. Two opposing groups formed: the Federalists, who supported the Constitution, and the Anti-Federalists, who did not. Many of those who did not support the Constitution believed there should be a bill of rights to protect individual rights.

Delaware became the first state to ratify it on December 7, 1787. When New Hampshire voted for ratification on June 21, 1788, the United States Constitution became the supreme law of the land. Four states ratified the document after it had become law: Virginia; New York; North Carolina; and Rhode Island, which didn't ratify the document until May 29, 1790.

Think About It

1. Use your deductive-thinking skills to figure out why the Constitution became the supreme law of the land when New Hampshire ratified it.

2. Look at the image below. Use it to explain why James Madison is often called "Father of the United States Constitution."

3. Several Patriots such as Thomas Jefferson, Patrick Henry, and Sam Adams were against ratification of the Constitution as it was presented at the end of the Constitutional Convention. Why, do you think, did they oppose it?

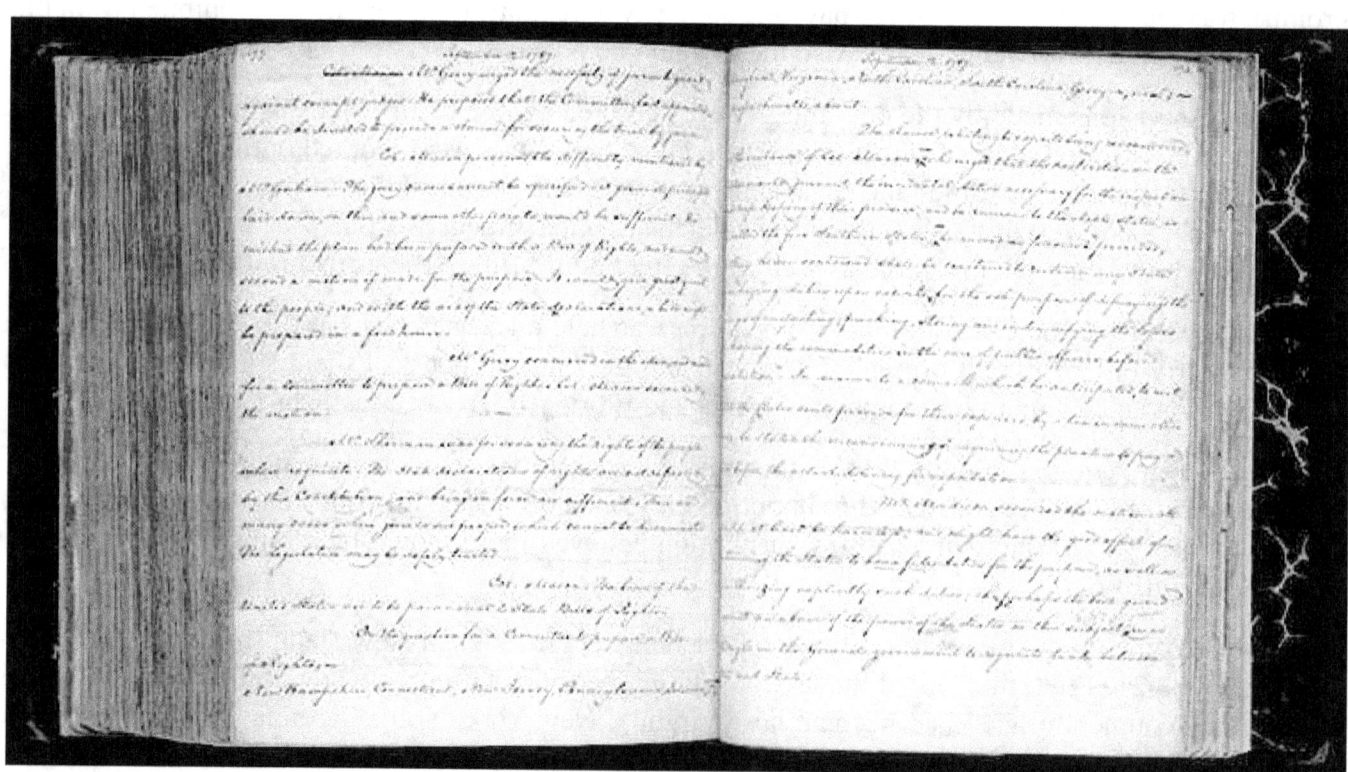

Madison's Notes from Notes of Debates in the Constitutional Convention
Source: Library of Congress

Preamble to the U.S. Constitution

We the People of the United States, in Order to form a more perfect Union, establish Justice, insure domestic Tranquility, provide for the common defence, promote the general Welfare, and secure the Blessings of Liberty to ourselves and our Posterity, do ordain and establish this Constitution for the United States of America.

4. Rewrite the Preamble in your own words.

The Federalist Papers
Promoting the U.S. Constitution

Background Information

The Federalist, later known as *The Federalist Papers,* is a collection of 85 essays written by Alexander Hamilton, James Madison, and John Jay. No one knows for sure, but it is generally believed that Hamilton wrote 52, Madison 28, and Jay 5. All three authors used the pseudonym Publius, and their identities were kept secret.

One purpose of the essays was to provide information about what was in the Constitution, which had been created at the Constitutional Convention. Another was to provide reasons why ratification of the document should be supported. The essays were originally written as a series of letters to New York newspapers: *The Independent Journal, The New York Packet,* and *The Daily Advertiser.* In 1788 they were published in book format.

In writing these essays, the authors tried to address all the objections people expressed regarding the provisions of the document. One of the misgivings was the belief that it would result in a tyrannical government. Many feared that it would take away states' rights and would interfere with personal liberties.

The three men who authored the essays were Federalists. They held the view that the most important concern was to protect the Union and that ratification was the best way to achieve that goal. The authors explained that the checks and balances and the clearly stated, limited powers of the central government would protect the rights of the states. They tried to make people understand why under the Articles of Confederation the government was not strong enough to hold the Union together.

Many Anti-Federalists, those who opposed the new Constitution, were against ratification of the document because it did not have a bill of rights. They wanted individual rights to be more explicitly addressed. Alexander Hamilton tried to convince them that the Constitution already protected the rights of individuals and that a separate bill of rights was unnecessary.

It is uncertain whether or not *The Federalist* had any influence on ratification. What is known, however, is that the essays were then and continue to be a valuable source for the interpretation and understanding of the intent of the founding fathers who drafted the United States Constitution.

Alexander Hamilton
Portrait By John Trumbull

John Jay
Portrait By Gilbert Stuart

James Madison
Portrait By John Vanderlyn

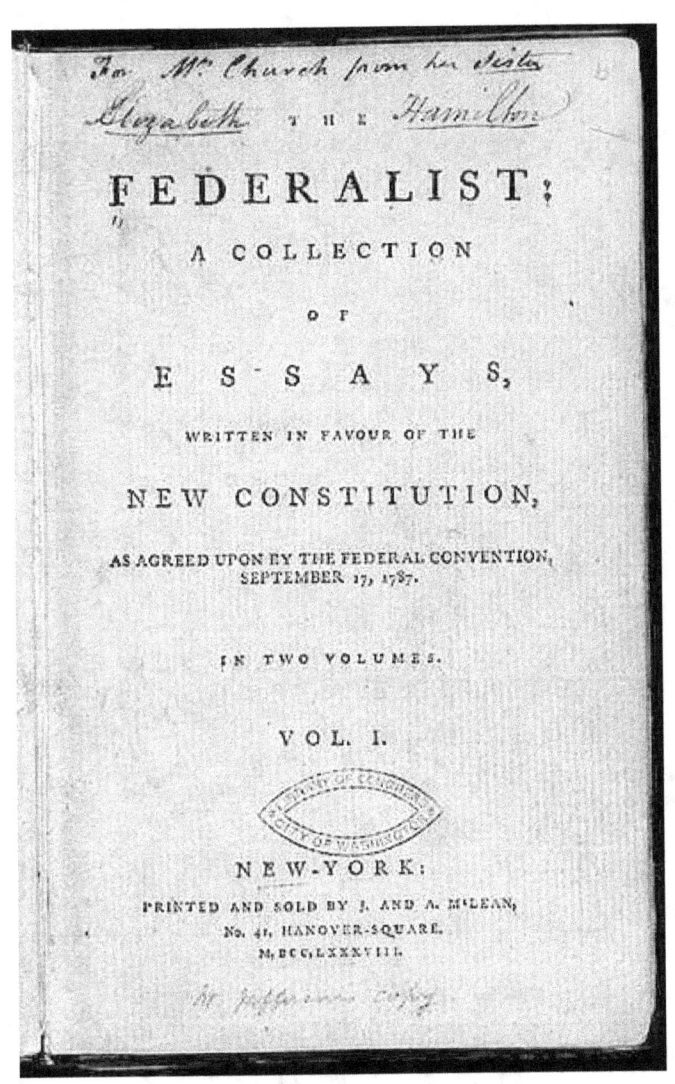

Think About It

1. In your opinion, why did the men use a pseudonym?

2. Research Publius. In your opinion, why did the men choose Publius as their pseudonym?

3. Hamilton and Jay were from New York, and that is where they did most of their speaking out in favor of the ratification of the Constitution. Madison was from Virginia and did most of his campaigning in that state.

Use this information to evaluate the influence of *The Federalist* on ratification of the U.S. Constitution.

4. Thomas Jefferson, Patrick Henry, Samuel Adams, and some other great Patriots were Anti-Federalists. Why, do you think, did they oppose the U.S. Constitution in the form presented to them by the Constitutional Convention?

5. What can we infer from the handwritten notes at the top and the body?

Think About It: Advertisement

1. What is the purpose of the ad?

2. According to the ad, what is *The Federalist*?

3. In what form will it be? Explain.

4. Why will some copies be more expensive than others?

5. Research and explain the meaning of Philo-Publius.

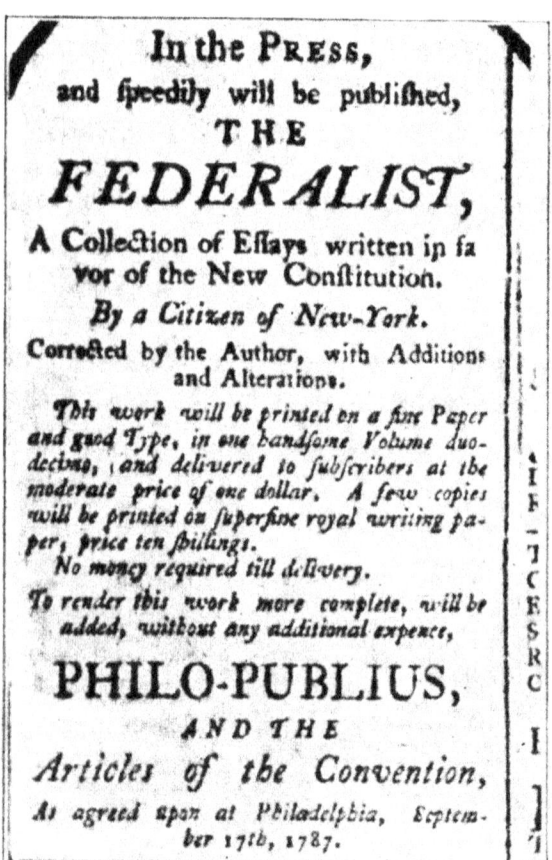

An advertisement for *The Federalist*, 1787, using the pseudonym "Philo-Publius"

In the PRESS,
and speedily will be published,
THE
FEDERALIST,
A Collection of Essays written in fa
vor of the New Constitution.
By a Citizen of New-York.
Corrected by the Author, with Additions
and Alterations.

The work will be printed on a fine Paper and good Type, in one handsome Volume duo-decimo, and delivered to subscribers at the moderate price of one dollar. A few copies will be printed on superfine royal writing paper, price ten shillings.
No money required till delivery.
To render this work more complete, will be added, without any additional expence,

PHILO-PUBLIUS,
AND THE
Articles of the Convention,
As agreed upon at Philadelphia, September 17th, 1787.

The United States Constitution
Signing the Document

Background Information

Nine states were required to ratify the Constitution in order for it to become the law of the land. Delaware became the first state to ratify it on December 7, 1787. New Hampshire was the ninth state to ratify it. When it voted for ratification on June 21, 1788, the United States Constitution became the supreme law of the land. Four states ratified the document after it had become law: Virginia, New York, North Carolina, and Rhode Island.

The document was signed on September 17, 1787.

This image is a reproduction of Howard Chandler Christy's 1940 painting "Scene at the Signing of the Constitution of the United States." This work was purchased from the painter in 1819 and now hangs in the United States Capitol building.

See how many founding fathers you can identify.

The key is found on the next page.

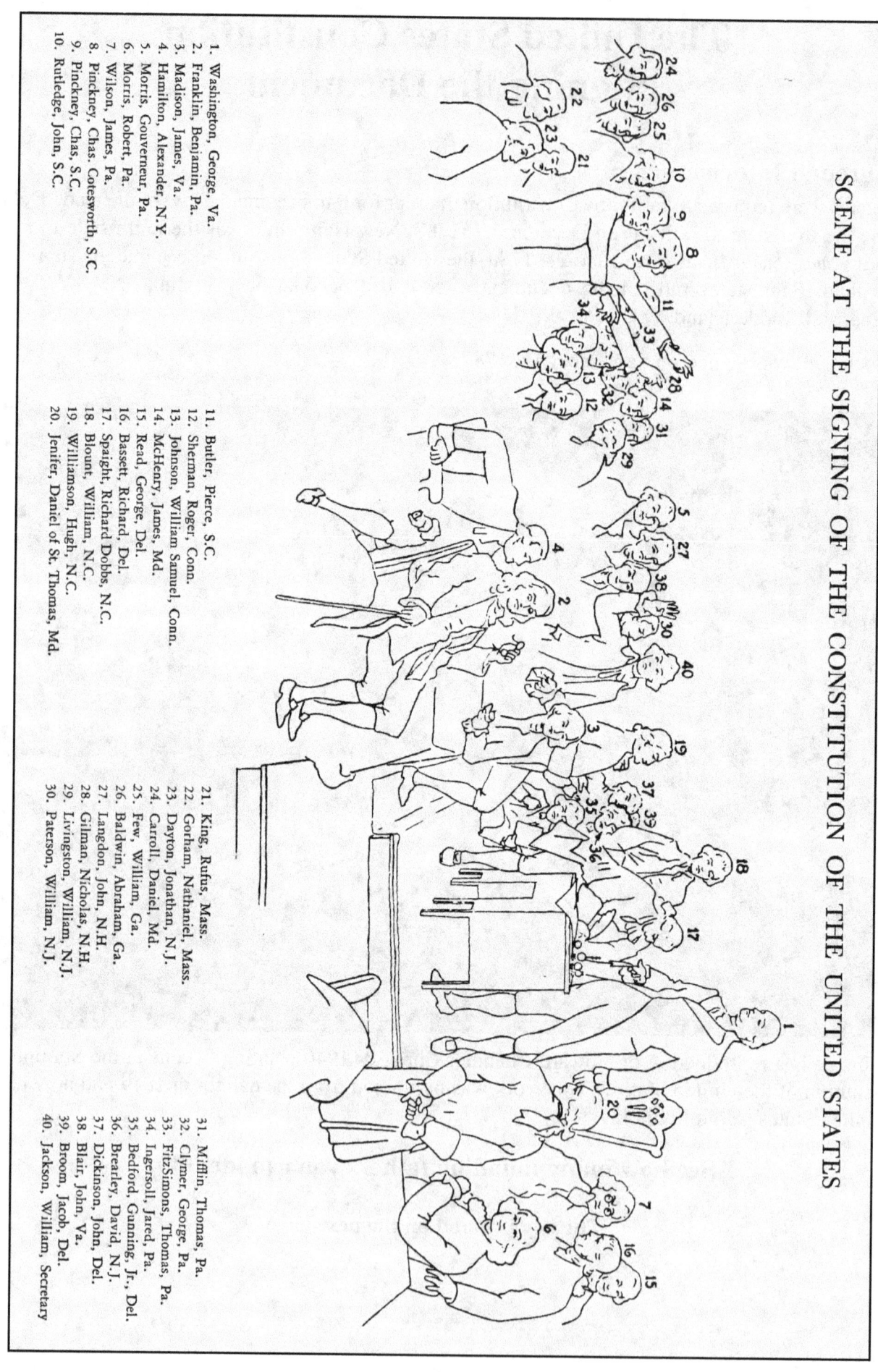

SCENE AT THE SIGNING OF THE CONSTITUTION OF THE UNITED STATES

1. Washington, George, Va.
2. Franklin, Benjamin, Pa.
3. Madison, James, Va.
4. Hamilton, Alexander, N.Y.
5. Morris, Gouverneur, Pa.
6. Morris, Robert, Pa.
7. Wilson, James, Pa.
8. Pinckney, Chas Cotesworth, S.C.
9. Pinckney, Chas, S.C.
10. Rutledge, John, S.C.
11. Butler, Pierce, S.C.
12. Sherman, Roger, Conn.
13. Johnson, William Samuel, Conn.
14. McHenry, James, Md.
15. Read, George, Del.
16. Bassett, Richard, Del.
17. Spaight, Richard Dobbs, N.C.
18. Blount, William, N.C.
19. Williamson, Hugh, N.C.
20. Jenifer, Daniel of St. Thomas, Md.
21. King, Rufus, Mass.
22. Gorham, Nathaniel, Mass.
23. Dayton, Jonathan, N.J.
24. Carroll, Daniel, Md.
25. Few, William, Ga.
26. Baldwin, Abraham, Ga.
27. Langdon, John, N.H.
28. Gilman, Nicholas, N.H.
29. Livingston, William, N.J.
30. Paterson, William, N.J.
31. Mifflin, Thomas, Pa.
32. Clymer, George, Pa.
33. FitzSimons, Thomas, Pa.
34. Ingersoll, Jared, Pa.
35. Bedford, Gunning, Jr., Del.
36. Brearley, David, N.J.
37. Dickinson, John, Del.
38. Blair, John, Va.
39. Broom, Jacob, Del.
40. Jackson, William, Secretary

74 *Using Primary Sources to Teach U.S. History: War to Constitution* © **Barbara M. Peller**

President George Washington First Inauguration

Background Information

George Washington was inaugurated as the first President of the United States on April 30, 1789. The ceremony took place on the balcony of Federal Hall in New York City. At that time New York City was the capital of the United States, and Federal Hall was where Congress met.

Washington was viewed by many as a hero, and a large crowd had gathered below to witness the momentous event. When Vice-President John Adams announced that it was time, the ceremony began. President Washington swore to "preserve, protect, and defend the Constitution of the United States."

When the official ceremony was over, President Washington and the members of Congress went inside to the Senate Chamber, where the President would deliver his prepared speech to Congress. In it he expressed the anxieties he felt knowing that everything he did would be seen as setting a precedent. He stressed the responsibility he shared with Congress to preserve the republican form of government and to protect our liberties.

From there President Washington, Vice-President Adams, and members of the Senate and House of Representative took a short walk to St. Paul's Chapel for a service officiated by the Right Rev. Samuel Provoost, the newly appointed chaplain of the United States Senate and first Episcopal bishop of New York.

Source: The U.S. National Archives and Records Administration

TRANSCRIPTION OF THE FIRST PART OF WASHINGTON'S INAUGURAL ADDRESS

Fellow Citizens of the Senate and the House of Representatives

"Among the vicissitudes incident to life, no event could have filled me with greater anxieties than that of which the notification was transmitted by your order, and received on the fourteenth day of the present month. On the one hand, I was summoned by my Country, whose voice I can never hear but with veneration and love, from a retreat which I had chosen with the fondest predilection, and, in my flattering hopes, with an immutable decision, as the asylum of my declining years: a retreat which was rendered every day more necessary as well as more dear to me, by the addition of habit to inclination, and of frequent interruptions in my health to the gradual waste committed on it by time. On the other hand, the magnitude and difficulty of the trust to which the voice of my Country called me, being sufficient to awaken in the wisest and most experienced of her citizens, a distrustful...."

Think About It

1. Washington began by saying, "Among the vicissitudes incident to life, no event could have filled me with greater anxieties than that of which the notification was transmitted by your order;" Define *vicissitude*. Do you think this was an appropriate term?

2. Describe the mixed feelings President Washington expressed in this excerpt.

3. Below is a continuation of the excerpt (beginning with the start of the last sentence) seen in the primary source. Read it and explain in your own words what Washington is expressing.

"On the other hand, the magnitude and difficulty of the trust to which the voice of my Country called me, being sufficient to awaken in the wisest and most experienced of her citizens, a distrustful scrutiny into his qualifications, could not but overwhelm with dispondence, one, who, inheriting inferior endowments from nature and unpractised in the duties of civil administration ought to be peculiarly conscious of his own deficiencies....All I dare hope, is, that, if in executing this task I have been too much swayed by a grateful remembrance of former instances, or by an affectionate sensibility to this transcendent proof, of the confidence of my fellow-citizens; and have thence too little consulted my incapacity as well as disinclination for the weighty and untried cares before me; my error will be palliated by the motives which misled me, and its consequences be judged by my Country, with someshare of the partiality in which they originated."

4. In the following excerpt President Washington alluded to the Fifth Article of the Constitution. What issue does this article address? What did the President want Congress to consider?

"Besides the ordinary objects submitted to your care, it will remain with your judgment to decide, how far an exercise of the occasional power delegated by the Fifth article of the Constitution is rendered expedient at the present juncture by the nature of objections which have been urged against the System, or by the degree of inquietude which has given birth to them. ...I shall again give way to my entire confidence in your discernment and pursuit of the public good: For I assure myself that whilst you carefully avoid every alteration which might endanger the benefits of an United and effective Government, or which ought to await the future lessons of experience; a reverence for the characteristic rights of freemen, and a regard for the public harmony, will sufficiently influence your deliberations on the question how far the former can be more impregnably fortified, or the latter be safely and advantageously promoted."

5. Read the following excerpt that comes near the end of his speech. Summarize the President's intent.

"To the preceeding observations I have one to add.... It concerns myself.... When I was first honoured with a call into the Service of my Country, then on the eve of an arduous struggle for its liberties, the light in which I contemplated my duty required that I should renounce every pecuniary compensation. From this resolution I have in no instance departed. And being still under the impressions which produced it, I must decline as inapplicable to myself, any share in the personal emoluments, which may be indispensably included in a permanent provision for the Executive Department; and must accordingly pray that the pecuniary estimates for the Station in which I am placed, may, during my continuance in it, be limited to such actual expenditures as the public good may be thought to require."

The Bill of Rights
The First Ten Amendments to the Constitution

Background Information

As the Constitutional Convention neared completion, George Mason of Virginia and Elbridge Gerry of Massachusetts proposed that the Constitution be "prefaced with a bill of rights." Most of the delegates were against the idea, however. On September 12, 1787, the proposal was unanimously rejected. The reason given was that it was unnecessary—that the document as it was written was sufficient to protect individual rights.

On September 25, 1789, the Joint Resolution of the First Congress of the United States proposed 12 amendments to the Constitution. Ten of the proposed 12 amendments were ratified by 3/4 of the state legislatures on December 15, 1791. These ratified articles (Articles 3–12) became the first 10 amendments of the Constitution, or the U.S. Bill of Rights. In 1992, 203 years after it was proposed, Article 2 was ratified as the 27th Amendment to the Constitution. Article 1 was never ratified.

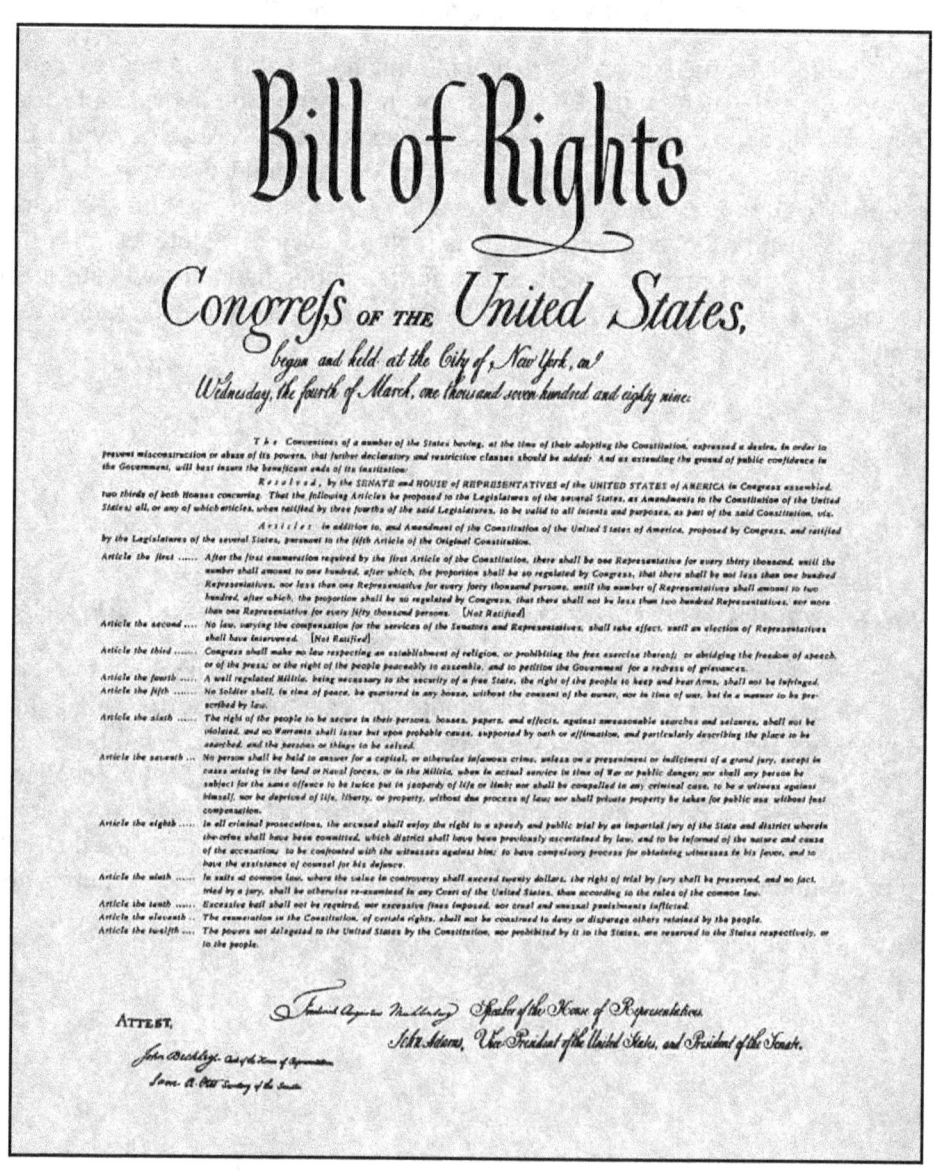

Think About It

1. What issue does 27th amendment to the Constitution address?

2. Put the ten amendments included in the Bill of Rights into your own words.

Transcriptions of Select Documents

The spelling and punctuation of the original documents are retained.

Transcription of The Declaration of Independence

Note: The following text is a transcription of the Stone Engraving of the parchment Declaration of Independence (the document on display in the Rotunda at the National Archives Museum.)

In Congress, July 4, 1776.

The unanimous Declaration of the thirteen united States of America, When in the Course of human events, it becomes necessary for one people to dissolve the political bands which have connected them with another, and to assume among the powers of the earth, the separate and equal station to which the Laws of Nature and of Nature's God entitle them, a decent respect to the opinions of mankind requires that they should declare the causes which impel them to the separation.

We hold these truths to be self-evident, that all men are created equal, that they are endowed by their Creator with certain unalienable Rights, that among these are Life, Liberty and the pursuit of Happiness.--That to secure these rights, Governments are instituted among Men, deriving their just powers from the consent of the governed, --That whenever any Form of Government becomes destructive of these ends, it is the Right of the People to alter or to abolish it, and to institute new Government, laying its foundation on such principles and organizing its powers in such form, as to them shall seem most likely to effect their Safety and Happiness. Prudence, indeed, will dictate that Governments long established should not be changed for light and transient causes; and accordingly all experience hath shewn, that mankind are more disposed to suffer, while evils are sufferable, than to right themselves by abolishing the forms to which they are accustomed. But when a long train of abuses and usurpations, pursuing invariably the same Object evinces a design to reduce them under absolute Despotism, it is their right, it is their duty, to throw off such Government, and to provide new Guards for their future security.--Such has been the patient sufferance of these Colonies; and such is now the necessity which constrains them to alter their former Systems of Government. The history of the present King of Great Britain is a history of repeated injuries and usurpations, all having in direct object the establishment of an absolute Tyranny over these States. To prove this, let Facts be submitted to a candid world.

He has refused his Assent to Laws, the most wholesome and necessary for the public good.

He has forbidden his Governors to pass Laws of immediate and pressing importance, unless suspended in their operation till his Assent should be obtained; and when so suspended, he has utterly neglected to attend to them.

He has refused to pass other Laws for the accommodation of large districts of people, unless those people would relinquish the right of Representation in the Legislature, a right inestimable to them and formidable to tyrants only.

He has called together legislative bodies at places unusual, uncomfortable, and distant from the depository of their public Records, for the sole purpose of fatiguing them into compliance with his measures.

He has dissolved Representative Houses repeatedly, for opposing with manly firmness his invasions on the rights of the people.

He has refused for a long time, after such dissolutions, to cause others to be elected; whereby the Legislative powers, incapable of Annihilation, have returned to the People at large for their exercise; the State remaining in the mean time exposed to all the dangers of invasion from without, and convulsions within.

He has endeavoured to prevent the population of these States; for that purpose obstructing the Laws for Naturalization of Foreigners; refusing to pass others to encourage their migrations hither, and raising the conditions of new Appropriations of Lands.

He has obstructed the Administration of Justice, by refusing his Assent to Laws for establishing Judiciary powers.

He has made Judges dependent on his Will alone, for the tenure of their offices, and the amount and payment of their salaries.

He has erected a multitude of New Offices, and sent hither swarms of Officers to harrass our people, and eat out their substance.

He has kept among us, in times of peace, Standing Armies without the Consent of our legislatures.

He has affected to render the Military independent of and superior to the Civil power.

He has combined with others to subject us to a jurisdiction foreign to our constitution, and unacknowledged by our laws; giving his Assent to their Acts of pretended Legislation.

For Quartering large bodies of armed troops among us:

For protecting them, by a mock Trial, from punishment for any Murders which they should commit on the Inhabitants of these States:

For cutting off our Trade with all parts of the world:

For imposing Taxes on us without our Consent:

For depriving us in many cases, of the benefits of Trial by Jury:

For transporting us beyond Seas to be tried for pretended offences

For abolishing the free System of English Laws in a neighbouring Province, establishing therein an Arbitrary government, and enlarging its Boundaries so as to render it at once an example and fit instrument for introducing the same absolute rule into these Colonies:

For taking away our Charters, abolishing our most valuable Laws, and altering fundamentally the Forms of our Governments:

For suspending our own Legislatures, and declaring themselves invested with power to legislate for us in all cases whatsoever.

He has abdicated Government here, by declaring us out of his Protection and waging War against us.

He has plundered our seas, ravaged our Coasts, burnt our towns, and destroyed the lives of our people.

He is at this time transporting large Armies of foreign Mercenaries to compleat the works of death, desolation and tyranny, already begun with circumstances of Cruelty & perfidy scarcely paralleled in the most barbarous ages, and totally unworthy the Head of a civilized nation.

He has constrained our fellow Citizens taken Captive on the high Seas to bear Arms against their Country, to become the executioners of their friends and Brethren, or to fall themselves by their Hands.

He has excited domestic insurrections amongst us, and has endeavoured to bring on the inhabitants of our frontiers, the merciless Indian Savages, whose known rule of warfare, is an undistinguished destruction of all ages, sexes and conditions.

In every stage of these Oppressions We have Petitioned for Redress in the most humble terms: Our repeated Petitions have been answered only by repeated injury. A Prince whose character is thus marked by every act which may define a Tyrant, is unfit to be the ruler of a free people.

Nor have We been wanting in attentions to our Brittish brethren. We have warned them from time to time of attempts by their legislature to extend an unwarrantable jurisdiction over us. We have reminded them of the circumstances of our emigration and settlement here. We have appealed to their native justice and magnanimity, and we have conjured them by the ties of our common kindred to disavow these usurpations, which, would inevitably interrupt our connections and correspondence. They too have been deaf to the voice of justice and of consanguinity. We must, therefore, acquiesce in the necessity, which denounces our Separation, and hold them, as we hold the rest of mankind, Enemies in War, in Peace Friends.

We, therefore, the Representatives of the united States of America, in General Congress, Assembled, appealing to the Supreme Judge of the world for the rectitude of our intentions, do, in the Name, and by Authority of the good People of these Colonies, solemnly publish and declare, That these United Colonies are, and of Right ought to be Free and Independent States; that they are Absolved from all Allegiance to the British Crown, and that all political connection between them and the State of Great Britain, is and ought to be totally dissolved; and that as Free and Independent States, they have full Power to levy War, conclude Peace, contract Alliances, establish Commerce, and to do all other Acts and Things which Independent States may of right do. And for the support of this Declaration, with a firm reliance on the protection of divine Providence, we mutually pledge to each other our Lives, our Fortunes and our sacred Honor.

Transcription of The Articles of Confederation

To all to whom these Presents shall come, we the undersigned Delegates of the States affixed to our Names send greeting.

Articles of Confederation and perpetual Union between the states of New Hampshire, Massachusetts-bay Rhode Island and Providence Plantations, Connecticut, New York, New Jersey, Pennsylvania, Delaware, Maryland, Virginia, North Carolina, South Carolina and Georgia.

I. The Stile of this Confederacy shall be "The United States of America."

II. Each state retains its sovereignty, freedom, and independence, and every power, jurisdiction, and right, which is not by this Confederation expressly delegated to the United States, in Congress assembled.

III. The said States hereby severally enter into a firm league of friendship with each other, for their common defense, the security of their liberties, and their mutual and general welfare, binding themselves to assist each other, against all force offered to, or attacks made upon them, or any of them, on account of religion, sovereignty, trade, or any other pretense whatever.

IV. The better to secure and perpetuate mutual friendship and intercourse among the people of the different States in this Union, the free inhabitants of each of these States, paupers, vagabonds, and fugitives from justice excepted, shall be entitled to all privileges and immunities of free citizens in the several States; and the people of each State shall free ingress and regress to and from any other State, and shall enjoy therein all the privileges of trade and commerce, subject to the same duties, impositions, and restrictions as the inhabitants thereof respectively, provided that such restrictions shall not extend so far as to prevent the removal of property imported into any State, to any other State, of which the owner is an inhabitant; provided also that no imposition, duties or restriction shall be laid by any State, on the property of the United States, or either of them.

If any person guilty of, or charged with, treason, felony, or other high misdemeanor in any State, shall flee from justice, and be found in any of the United States, he shall, upon demand of the Governor or executive power of the State from which he fled, be delivered up and removed to the State having jurisdiction of his offense.

Full faith and credit shall be given in each of these States to the records, acts, and judicial proceedings of the courts and magistrates of every other State.

V. For the most convenient management of the general interests of the United States, delegates shall be annually appointed in such manner as the legislatures of each State shall direct, to meet in Congress on the first Monday in November, in every year, with a power reserved to each State to recall its delegates, or any of them, at any time within the year, and to send others in their stead for the remainder of the year.

No State shall be represented in Congress by less than two, nor more than seven members; and no person shall be capable of being a delegate for more than three years in any term of six years; nor shall any person, being a delegate, be capable of holding any office under the United States, for which he, or another for his benefit, receives any salary, fees or emolument of any kind.

Each State shall maintain its own delegates in a meeting of the States, and while they act as members of the committee of the States.

In determining questions in the United States in Congress assembled, each State shall have one vote.

Freedom of speech and debate in Congress shall not be impeached or questioned in any court or place out of Congress, and the members of Congress shall be protected in their persons from arrests or imprisonments, during the time of their going to and from, and attendence on Congress, except for treason, felony, or breach of the peace.

VI. No State, without the consent of the United States in Congress assembled, shall send any embassy to, or receive any embassy from, or enter into any conference, agreement, alliance or treaty with any King, Prince or State; nor shall any person holding any office of profit or trust under the United States, or any of them, accept any present, emolument, office or title of any kind whatever from any King, Prince or foreign State; nor shall the United States in Congress assembled, or any of them, grant any title of nobility.

No two or more States shall enter into any treaty, confederation or alliance whatever between them, without the consent of the United States in Congress assembled, specifying accurately the purposes for which the same is to be entered into, and how long it shall continue.

No State shall lay any imposts or duties, which may interfere with any stipulations in treaties, entered into by the United States in Congress assembled, with any King, Prince or State, in pursuance of any treaties already proposed by Congress, to the courts of France and Spain.

No vessel of war shall be kept up in time of peace by any State, except such number only, as shall be deemed necessary by the United States in Congress assembled, for the defense of such State, or its trade; nor shall any body of forces be kept up by any State in time of peace, except such number only, as in the judgement of the United States in Congress assembled, shall be deemed requisite to garrison the forts necessary for the defense of such State; but every State shall always keep up a well-regulated and disciplined militia, sufficiently armed and accoutered, and shall provide and constantly have ready for use, in public stores, a due number of filed pieces and tents, and a proper quantity of arms, ammunition and camp equipage.

No State shall engage in any war without the consent of the United States in Congress assembled, unless such State be actually invaded by enemies, or shall have received certain advice of a resolution being formed by some nation of Indians to invade such State, and the danger is so imminent as not to admit of a delay till the United States in Congress assembled can be consulted; nor shall any State grant commissions to any ships or vessels of war, nor letters of marque or reprisal, except it be after a declaration of war by the United States in Congress assembled, and then only against the Kingdom or State and the subjects thereof, against which war has been so declared, and under such regulations as shall be established by the United States in Congress assembled, unless such State be infested by pirates, in which case vessels of war may be fitted out for that occasion, and kept so long as the danger shall continue, or until the United States in Congress assembled shall determine otherwise.

VII. When land forces are raised by any State for the common defense, all officers of or under the rank of colonel, shall be appointed by the legislature of each State respectively, by whom such forces shall be raised, or in such manner as such State shall direct, and all vacancies shall be filled up by the State which first made the appointment.

VIII. All charges of war, and all other expenses that shall be incurred for the common defense or general welfare, and allowed by the United States in Congress assembled, shall be defrayed out of a common treasury, which shall be supplied by the several States in proportion to the value of all land within each State, granted or surveyed for any person, as such land and the buildings and improvements thereon shall be estimated according to such mode as the United States in Congress assembled, shall from time to time direct and appoint.

The taxes for paying that proportion shall be laid and levied by the authority and direction of the legislatures of the several States within the time agreed upon by the United States in Congress assembled.

IX. The United States in Congress assembled, shall have the sole and exclusive right and power of determining on peace and war, except in the cases mentioned in the sixth article -- of sending and receiving ambassadors -- entering into treaties and alliances, provided that no treaty of commerce shall be made whereby the legislative power of the respective States shall be restrained from imposing such imposts and duties on foreigners, as their own people are subjected to, or from prohibiting the exportation or importation of any species of goods or commodities whatsoever -- of establishing rules for deciding in all cases, what captures on land or water shall be legal, and in what manner prizes taken by land or naval forces in the service of the United States shall be divided or appropriated -- of granting letters of marque and reprisal in times of peace -- appointing courts for the trial of piracies and felonies committed on the high seas and establishing courts for receiving and determining finally appeals in all cases of captures, provided that no member of Congress shall be appointed a judge of any of the said courts.

The United States in Congress assembled shall also be the last resort on appeal in all disputes and differences now subsisting or that hereafter may arise between two or more States concerning boundary, jurisdiction or any other causes whatever; which authority shall always be exercised in the manner following. Whenever the legislative or executive authority or lawful agent of any State in controversy with another shall present a petition to Congress stating the matter in question and praying for a hearing, notice thereof shall be given by order of Congress to the legislative or executive authority of the other State in controversy, and a day assigned for the appearance of the parties by their lawful agents, who shall then be directed to appoint by joint consent, commissioners or judges to constitute a court for hearing and determining the matter in question: but if they cannot agree, Congress shall name three persons out of each of the United States, and from the list of such persons each party shall alternately strike out one, the petitioners beginning, until the number shall be reduced to thirteen; and from that number not less than seven, nor more than nine names as Congress shall direct, shall in the presence of Congress be drawn out by lot, and the persons whose names shall be so drawn or any five of them, shall be commissioners or judges, to hear and finally determine the controversy, so always as a major part of the judges who shall hear the cause shall agree in the determination: and if either party shall neglect to attend at the day appointed, without showing reasons, which Congress shall judge sufficient, or being present shall refuse to strike, the Congress shall proceed to nominate three persons out of each State, and the secretary of Congress shall strike in behalf of such party absent or refusing; and the judgement and sentence of the court to be appointed, in the manner before prescribed, shall be final and conclusive; and if any of the parties shall refuse to submit to the authority of such court, or to appear or defend their claim or cause, the court shall nevertheless proceed to pronounce sentence, or judgement, which shall in like manner be final and decisive, the judgement or sentence and other proceedings being in either case transmitted to Congress, and lodged among the acts of Congress for the security of the parties concerned: provided that every commissioner, before he sits in judgement, shall take an oath to be administered by one of the judges of the supreme or superior court of the State, where the cause shall be tried, 'well and truly to hear and determine the matter in question, according to the best of his judgement, without favor, affection or hope of reward': provided also, that no State shall be deprived of territory for the benefit of the United States.

All controversies concerning the private right of soil claimed under different grants of two or more States, whose jurisdictions as they may respect such lands, and the States which passed such grants are adjusted, the said grants or either of them being at the same time claimed to have originated antecedent to such settlement of jurisdiction, shall on the petition of either party to the Congress of the United States, be finally determined as near as may be in the same manner as is before prescribed for deciding disputes respecting territorial jurisdiction between different States.

The United States in Congress assembled shall also have the sole and exclusive right and power of regulating the alloy and value of coin struck by their own authority, or by that of the respective States -- fixing the standards of weights and measures throughout the United States -- regulating the trade and managing all affairs with the Indians, not members of any of the States, provided that the legislative right of any State within its own limits be not infringed or violated -- establishing or regulating post offices from one State to another, throughout all the United States, and exacting such postage on the papers passing through the same as may be requisite to defray the expenses of the said office -- appointing all officers of the land forces, in the service of the United States, excepting regimental officers -- appointing all the officers of the naval forces, and commissioning all officers whatever in the service of the United States -- making rules for the government and regulation of the said land and naval forces, and directing their operations.

The United States in Congress assembled shall have authority to appoint a committee, to sit in the recess of Congress, to be denominated 'A Committee of the States', and to consist of one delegate from each State; and to appoint such other committees and civil officers as may be necessary for managing the general affairs of the United States under their direction -- to appoint one of their members to preside, provided that no person be allowed to serve in the office of president more than one year in any term of three years; to ascertain the necessary sums of money to be raised for the service of the United States, and to appropriate and apply the same for defraying the public expenses -- to borrow money, or emit bills on the credit of the United States, transmitting every half-year to the respective States an account of the sums of money so borrowed or emitted -- to build and equip a navy -- to agree upon the number of land forces, and to make requisitions from each State for its quota, in proportion to the number of white inhabitants in such State; which requisition shall be binding, and thereupon the legislature of each State shall appoint the regimental officers, raise the men and cloath, arm and equip them in a solid-like manner, at the expense of the United States; and the officers and men so cloathed, armed and equipped shall march to the place appointed, and within the time agreed on by the United States in Congress assembled. But if the United States in Congress assembled shall, on consideration of circumstances judge proper that any State should not raise men, or should raise a smaller number of men than the quota thereof, such extra number shall be raised, officered, cloathed, armed and equipped in the same manner as the quota of each State, unless the legislature of such State shall judge that such extra number cannot be safely spread out in the same, in which case they shall raise, officer, cloath, arm and equip as many of such extra number as they judge can be safely spared. And the officers and men so cloathed, armed, and equipped, shall march to the place appointed, and within the time agreed on by the United States in Congress assembled.

The United States in Congress assembled shall never engage in a war, nor grant letters of marque or reprisal in time of peace, nor enter into any treaties or alliances, nor coin money, nor regulate the value thereof, nor ascertain the sums and expenses necessary for the defense and welfare of the United States, or any of them, nor emit bills, nor borrow money on the credit of the United States, nor appropriate money, nor agree upon the number of vessels of war, to be built or purchased, or the number of land or sea forces to be raised, nor appoint a commander in chief of the army or navy, unless nine States assent to the same: nor shall a question on any other point, except for adjourning from day to day be determined, unless by the votes of the majority of the United States in Congress assembled.

The Congress of the United States shall have power to adjourn to any time within the year, and to any place within the United States, so that no period of adjournment be for a longer duration than the space of six months, and shall publish the journal of their proceedings monthly, except such parts thereof relating to treaties, alliances or military operations, as in their judgement require secrecy; and the yeas and nays of the delegates of each State on any question shall be entered on the journal, when it is desired by any delegates of a State, or any of them, at his or their request shall be furnished with a transcript of the said journal, except such parts as are above excepted, to lay before the legislatures of the several States.

X. The Committee of the States, or any nine of them, shall be authorized to execute, in the recess of Congress, such of the powers of Congress as the United States in Congress assembled, by the consent of the nine States, shall from time to time think expedient to vest them with; provided that no power be delegated to the said Committee, for the exercise of which, by the Articles of Confederation, the voice of nine States in the Congress of the United States assembled be requisite.

XI. Canada acceding to this confederation, and adjoining in the measures of the United States, shall be admitted into, and entitled to all the advantages of this Union; but no other colony shall be admitted into the same, unless such admission be agreed to by nine States.

XII. All bills of credit emitted, monies borrowed, and debts contracted by, or under the authority of Congress, before the assembling of the United States, in pursuance of the present confederation, shall be deemed and considered as a charge against the United States, for payment and satisfaction whereof the said United States, and the public faith are hereby solemnly pleged.

XIII. Every State shall abide by the determination of the United States in Congress assembled, on all questions which by this confederation are submitted to them. And the Articles of this Confederation shall be inviolably observed by every State, and the Union shall be perpetual; nor shall any alteration at any time hereafter be made in any of them; unless such alteration be agreed to in a Congress of the United States, and be afterwards confirmed by the legislatures of every State.

And Whereas it hath pleased the Great Governor of the World to incline the hearts of the legislatures we respectively represent in Congress, to approve of, and to authorize us to ratify the said Articles of Confederation and perpetual Union. Know Ye that we the undersigned delegates, by virtue of the power and authority to us given for that purpose, do by these presents, in the name and in behalf of our respective constituents, fully and entirely ratify and confirm each and every of the said Articles of Confederation and perpetual Union, and all and singular the matters and things therein contained: And we do further solemnly plight and engage the faith of our respective constituents, that they shall abide by the determinations of the United States in Congress assembled, on all questions, which by the said Confederation are submitted to them. And that the Articles thereof shall be inviolably observed by the States we respectively represent, and that the Union shall be perpetual.

In Witness whereof we have hereunto set our hands in Congress. Done at Philadelphia in the State of Pennsylvania the ninth day of July in the Year of our Lord One Thousand Seven Hundred and Seventy-Eight, and in the Third Year of the independence of America.

Agreed to by Congress 15 November 1777 In force after ratification by Maryland, 1 March 1781

© **Barbara M. Peller**

Transcription of Treaty of Paris (1783)

The Definitive Treaty of Peace 1783

In the Name of the most Holy & undivided Trinity.

It having pleased the Divine Providence to dispose the Hearts of the most Serene and most Potent Prince George the Third, by the Grace of God, King of Great Britain, France, and Ireland, Defender of the Faith, Duke of Brunswick and Lunebourg, Arch- Treasurer and Prince Elector of the Holy Roman Empire etc.. and of the United States of America, to forget all past Misunderstandings and Differences that have unhappily interrupted the good Correspondence and Friendship which they mutually wish to restore; and to establish such a beneficial and satisfactory Intercourse between the two countries upon the ground of reciprocal Advantages and mutual Convenience as may promote and secure to both perpetual Peace and Harmony; and having for this desirable End already laid the Foundation of Peace & Reconciliation by the Provisional Articles signed at Paris on the 30th of November 1782, by the Commissioners empowered on each Part, which Articles were agreed to be inserted in and constitute the Treaty of Peace proposed to be concluded between the Crown of Great Britain and the said United States, but which Treaty was not to be concluded until Terms of Peace should be agreed upon between Great Britain & France, and his Britannic Majesty should be ready to conclude such Treaty accordingly: and the treaty between Great Britain & France having since been concluded, his Britannic Majesty & the United States of America, in Order to carry into full Effect the Provisional Articles above mentioned, according to the Tenor thereof, have constituted & appointed, that is to say his Britannic Majesty on his Part, David Hartley, Esqr., Member of the Parliament of Great Britain, and the said United States on their Part, - stop point - John Adams, Esqr., late a Commissioner of the United States of America at the Court of Versailles, late Delegate in Congress from the State of Massachusetts, and Chief Justice of the said State, and Minister Plenipotentiary of the said United States to their High Mightinesses the States General of the United Netherlands; - stop point - Benjamin Franklin, Esqr., late Delegate in Congress from the State of Pennsylvania, President of the Convention of the said State, and Minister Plenipotentiary from the United States of America at the Court of Versailles; John Jay, Esqr., late President of Congress and Chief Justice of the state of New York, and Minister Plenipotentiary from the said United States at the Court of Madrid; to be Plenipotentiaries for the concluding and signing the Present Definitive Treaty; who after having reciprocally communicated their respective full Powers have agreed upon and confirmed the following Articles.

Article 1st:
His Brittanic Majesty acknowledges the said United States, viz., New Hampshire, Massachusetts Bay, Rhode Island and Providence Plantations, Connecticut, New York, New Jersey, Pennsylvania, Delaware, Maryland, Virginia, North Carolina, South Carolina and Georgia, to be free sovereign and Independent States; that he treats with them as such, and for himself his Heirs & Successors, relinquishes all claims to the Government, Propriety, and Territorial Rights of the same and every Part thereof..

Article 2d:
And that all Disputes which might arise in future on the subject of the Boundaries of the said United States may be prevented, it is hereby agreed and declared, that the following are and shall be their Boundaries, viz.; from the Northwest Angle of Nova Scotia, viz., that Angle which is formed by a Line drawn due North from the Source of St. Croix River to the Highlands; along the said Highlands which divide those Rivers that empty themselves into the river St. Lawrence, from those which fall into the Atlantic Ocean, to the northwesternmost Head of Connecticut River; Thence down along the middle of that River to the forty-fifth Degree of North Latitude; From thence by a Line due West on said Latitude until it strikes the River Iroquois or Cataraquy; Thence along the middle of said River into Lake Ontario; through the Middle of said Lake until it strikes the Communication by Water between that Lake & Lake Erie; Thence along the middle of said Communication into Lake Erie, through the middle of said Lake until it arrives at the Water Communication between that lake & Lake Huron; Thence along the middle of said Water Communication into the Lake Huron, thence through the middle of said Lake to the Water Communication between that Lake and Lake Superior; thence through Lake Superior Northward of the Isles Royal & Phelipeaux to the Long Lake; Thence through the middle of said Long Lake and the Water Communication

between it & the Lake of the Woods, to the said Lake of the Woods; Thence through the said Lake to the most Northwestern Point thereof, and from thence on a due West Course to the river Mississippi; Thence by a Line to be drawn along the Middle of the said river Mississippi until it shall intersect the Northernmost Part of the thirty-first Degree of North Latitude, South, by a Line to be drawn due East from the Determination of the Line last mentioned in the Latitude of thirty-one Degrees of the Equator to the middle of the River Apalachicola or Catahouche; Thence along the middle thereof to its junction with the Flint River; Thence straight to the Head of Saint Mary's River, and thence down along the middle of Saint Mary's River to the Atlantic Ocean. East, by a Line to be drawn along the Middle of the river Saint Croix, from its Mouth in the Bay of Fundy to its Source, and from its Source directly North to the aforesaid Highlands, which divide the Rivers that fall into the Atlantic Ocean from those which fall into the river Saint Lawrence; comprehending all Islands within twenty Leagues of any Part of the Shores of the United States, and lying between Lines to be drawn due East from the Points where the aforesaid Boundaries between Nova Scotia on the one Part and East Florida on the other shall, respectively, touch the Bay of Fundy and the Atlantic Ocean, excepting such Islands as now are or heretofore have been within the limits of the said Province of Nova Scotia.

Article 3d:
It is agreed that the People of the United States shall continue to enjoy unmolested the Right to take Fish of every kind on the Grand Bank and on all the other Banks of Newfoundland, also in the Gulf of Saint Lawrence and at all other Places in the Sea, where the Inhabitants of both Countries used at any time heretofore to fish. And also that the Inhabitants of the United States shall have Liberty to take Fish of every Kind on such Part of the Coast of Newfoundland as British Fishermen shall use, (but not to dry or cure the same on that Island) And also on the Coasts, Bays & Creeks of all other of his Brittanic Majesty's Dominions in America; and that the American Fishermen shall have Liberty to dry and cure Fish in any of the unsettled Bays, Harbors, and Creeks of Nova Scotia, Magdalen Islands, and Labrador, so long as the same shall remain unsettled, but so soon as the same or either of them shall be settled, it shall not be lawful for the said Fishermen to dry or cure Fish at such Settlement without a previous Agreement for that purpose with the Inhabitants, Proprietors, or Possessors of the Ground.

Article 4th:
It is agreed that Creditors on either Side shall meet with no lawful Impediment to the Recovery of the full Value in Sterling Money of all bona fide Debts heretofore contracted.

Article 5th:
It is agreed that Congress shall earnestly recommend it to the Legislatures of the respective States to provide for the Restitution of all Estates, Rights, and Properties, which have been confiscated belonging to real British Subjects; and also of the Estates, Rights, and Properties of Persons resident in Districts in the Possession on his Majesty's Arms and who have not borne Arms against the said United States. And that Persons of any other Description shall have free Liberty to go to any Part or Parts of any of the thirteen United States and therein to remain twelve Months unmolested in their Endeavors to obtain the Restitution of such of their Estates – Rights & Properties as may have been confiscated. And that Congress shall also earnestly recommend to the several States a Reconsideration and Revision of all Acts or Laws regarding the Premises, so as to render the said Laws or Acts perfectly consistent not only with Justice and Equity but with that Spirit of Conciliation which on the Return of the Blessings of Peace should universally prevail. And that Congress shall also earnestly recommend to the several States that the Estates, Rights, and Properties of such last mentioned Persons shall be restored to them, they refunding to any Persons who may be now in Possession the Bona fide Price (where any has been given) which such Persons may have paid on purchasing any of the said Lands, Rights, or Properties since the Confiscation.

And it is agreed that all Persons who have any Interest in confiscated Lands, either by Debts, Marriage Settlements, or otherwise, shall meet with no lawful Impediment in the Prosecution of their just Rights.

Article 6th:
That there shall be no future Confiscations made nor any Prosecutions commenced against any Person or Persons for, or by Reason of the Part, which he or they may have taken in the present War, and that no Person shall on that Account suffer any future Loss or Damage, either in his Person, Liberty, or Property; and that those who may be in Confinement on such Charges at the Time of the Ratification of the Treaty in America shall be immediately set at Liberty, and the Prosecutions so commenced be discontinued.

Article 7th:
There shall be a firm and perpetual Peace between his Britanic Majesty and the said States, and between the Subjects of the one and the Citizens of the other, wherefore all Hostilities both by Sea and Land shall from henceforth cease: All prisoners on both Sides shall be set at Liberty, and his Britanic Majesty shall with all convenient speed, and without causing any Destruction, or carrying away any Negroes or other Property of the American inhabitants, withdraw all his Armies, Garrisons & Fleets from the said United States, and from every Post, Place and Harbour within the same; leaving in all Fortifications, the American Artillery that may be therein: And shall also Order & cause all Archives, Records, Deeds & Papers belonging to any of the said States, or their Citizens, which in the Course of the War may have fallen into the hands of his Officers, to be forthwith restored and delivered to the proper States and Persons to whom they belong.

Article 8th:
The Navigation of the river Mississippi, from its source to the Ocean, shall forever remain free and open to the Subjects of Great Britain and the Citizens of the United States.

Article 9th:
In case it should so happen that any Place or Territory belonging to great Britain or to the United States should have been conquered by the Arms of either from the other before the Arrival of the said Provisional Articles in America, it is agreed that the same shall be restored without Difficulty and without requiring any Compensation.

Article 10th:
The solemn Ratifications of the present Treaty expedited in good & due Form shall be exchanged between the contracting Parties in the Space of Six Months or sooner if possible to be computed from the Day of the Signature of the present Treaty. In witness whereof we the undersigned their Ministers Plenipotentiary have in their Name and in Virtue of our Full Powers, signed with our Hands the present Definitive Treaty, and caused the Seals of our Arms to be affixed thereto.

Done at Paris, this third day of September in the year of our Lord, one thousand seven hundred and eighty-three.

D HARTLEY (SEAL)
JOHN ADAMS (SEAL)
B FRANKLIN (SEAL)
JOHN JAY (SEAL)

Bill of Rights
Transcription of 1789 Joint Resolution

On September 25, 1789, the First Congress of the United States proposed 12 amendments to the Constitution.

Congress of the United States begun and held at the City of New-York, on Wednesday the fourth of March, one thousand seven hundred and eighty nine.

THE Conventions of a number of the States, having at the time of their adopting the Constitution, expressed a desire, in order to prevent misconstruction or abuse of its powers, that further declaratory and restrictive clauses should be added: And as extending the ground of public confidence in the Government, will best ensure the beneficent ends of its institution.

RESOLVED by the Senate and House of Representatives of the United States of America, in Congress assembled, two thirds of both Houses concurring, that the following Articles be proposed to the Legislatures of the several States, as amendments to the Constitution of the United States, all, or any of which Articles, when ratified by three fourths of the said Legislatures, to be valid to all intents and purposes, as part of the said Constitution; viz.

ARTICLES in addition to, and Amendment of the Constitution of the United States of America, proposed by Congress, and ratified by the Legislatures of the several States, pursuant to the fifth Article of the original Constitution.

Article the first... After the first enumeration required by the first article of the Constitution, there shall be one Representative for every thirty thousand, until the number shall amount to one hundred, after which the proportion shall be so regulated by Congress, that there shall be not less than one hundred Representatives, nor less than one Representative for every forty thousand persons, until the number of Representatives shall amount to two hundred; after which the proportion shall be so regulated by Congress, that there shall not be less than two hundred Representatives, nor more than one Representative for every fifty thousand persons.

Article the second... No law, varying the compensation for the services of the Senators and Representatives, shall take effect, until an election of Representatives shall have intervened.

Article the third... Congress shall make no law respecting an establishment of religion, or prohibiting the free exercise thereof; or abridging the freedom of speech, or of the press; or the right of the people peaceably to assemble, and to petition the Government for a redress of grievances.

Article the fourth... A well regulated Militia, being necessary to the security of a free State, the right of the people to keep and bear Arms, shall not be infringed.

Article the fifth... No Soldier shall, in time of peace be quartered in any house, without the consent of the Owner, nor in time of war, but in a manner to be prescribed by law.

Article the sixth... The right of the people to be secure in their persons, houses, papers, and effects, against unreasonable searches and seizures, shall not be violated, and no Warrants shall issue, but upon probable cause, supported by Oath or affirmation, and particularly describing the place to be searched, and the persons or things to be seized.

Article the seventh... No person shall be held to answer for a capital, or otherwise infamous crime, unless on a presentment or indictment of a Grand Jury, except in cases arising in the land or naval forces, or in the Militia, when in actual service in time of War or public danger; nor shall any person be subject for the same offence to be twice put in jeopardy of life or limb; nor shall be compelled in any criminal case to be a witness against himself, nor be deprived of life, liberty, or property, without due process of law; nor shall private property be taken for public use, without just compensation.

Article the eighth... In all criminal prosecutions, the accused shall enjoy the right to a speedy and public trial, by an impartial jury of the State and district wherein the crime shall have been committed, which district shall have been previously ascertained by law, and to be informed of the nature and cause of the accusation; to be confronted with the witnesses against him; to have compulsory process for obtaining witnesses in his favor, and to have the Assistance of Counsel for his defence.

Article the ninth... In suits at common law, where the value in controversy shall exceed twenty dollars, the right of trial by jury shall be preserved, and no fact tried by a jury, shall be otherwise re-examined in any Court of the United States, than according to the rules of the common law.

Article the tenth... Excessive bail shall not be required, nor excessive fines imposed, nor cruel and unusual punishments inflicted.

Article the eleventh... The enumeration in the Constitution, of certain rights, shall not be construed to deny or disparage others retained by the people.

Article the twelfth... The powers not delegated to the United States by the Constitution, nor prohibited by it to the States, are reserved to the States respectively, or to the people.

ATTEST,

Frederick Augustus Muhlenberg, Speaker of the House of Representatives
John Adams, Vice-President of the United States, and President of the Senate
John Beckley, Clerk of the House of Representatives.
Sam. A Otis Secretary of the Senate

Transcription of Washington's Inaugural Address 1789

[April 30, 1789]

Fellow Citizens of the Senate and the House of Representatives.

Among the vicissitudes incident to life, no event could have filled me with greater anxieties than that of which the notification was transmitted by your order, and received on the fourteenth day of the present month. On the one hand, I was summoned by my Country, whose voice I can never hear but with veneration and love, from a retreat which I had chosen with the fondest predilection, and, in my flattering hopes, with an immutable decision, as the asylum of my declining years: a retreat which was rendered every day more necessary as well as more dear to me, by the addition of habit to inclination, and of frequent interruptions in my health to the gradual waste committed on it by time. On the other hand, the magnitude and difficulty of the trust to which the voice of my Country called me, being sufficient to awaken in the wisest and most experienced of her citizens, a distrustful scrutiny into his qualifications, could not but overwhelm with dispondence, one, who, inheriting inferior endowments from nature and unpractised in the duties of civil administration, ought to be peculiarly conscious of his own deficiencies. In this conflict of emotions, all I dare aver, is, that it has been my faithful study to collect my duty from a just appreciation of every circumstance, by which it might be affected. All I dare hope, is, that, if in executing this task I have been too much swayed by a grateful remembrance of former instances, or by an affectionate sensibility to this transcendent proof, of the confidence of my fellow-citizens; and have thence too little consulted my incapacity as well as disinclination for the weighty and untried cares before me; my error will be palliated by the motives which misled me, and its consequences be judged by my Country, with some share of the partiality in which they originated.

Such being the impressions under which I have, in obedience to the public summons, repaired to the present station; it would be peculiarly improper to omit in this first official Act, my fervent supplications to that Almighty Being who rules over the Universe, who presides in the Councils of Nations, and whose providential aids can supply every human defect, that his benediction may consecrate to the liberties and happiness of the People of the United States, a Government instituted by themselves for these essential purposes: and may enable every instrument employed in its administration to execute with success, the functions allotted to his charge. In tendering this homage to the Great Author of every public and private good I assure myself that it expresses your sentiments not less than my own; nor those of my fellow-citizens at large, less than either. No People can be bound to acknowledge and adore the invisible hand, which conducts the Affairs of men more than the People of the United States. Every step, by which they have advanced to the character of an independent nation, seems to have been distinguished by some token of providential agency. And in the important revolution just accomplished in the system of their United Government, the tranquil deliberations and voluntary consent of so many distinct communities, from which the event has resulted, cannot be compared with the means by which most Governments have been established, without some return of pious gratitude along with an humble anticipation of the future blessings which the past seem to presage. These reflections, arising out of the present crisis, have forced themselves too strongly on my mind to be suppressed. You will join with me I trust in thinking, that there are none under the influence of which, the proceedings of a new and free Government can more auspiciously commence.

By the article establishing the Executive Department, it is made the duty of the President "to recommend to your consideration, such measures as he shall judge necessary and expedient." The circumstances under which I now meet you, will acquit me from entering into that subject, farther than to refer to the Great Constitutional Charter under which you are assembled; and which, in defining your powers, designates the objects to which your attention is to be given. It will be more consistent with those circumstances, and far more congenial with the feelings which actuate me, to substitute, in place of a recommendation of particular measures, the tribute that is due to the talents, the rectitude, and the patriotism which adorn the characters selected to devise and adopt them. In these honorable qualifications, I behold the surest pledges, that as on one side, no local prejudices, or attachments; no separate views, nor party animosities, will misdirect the comprehensive and equal eye which ought to watch over this great assemblage of communities and interests: so, on another, that the foundations of our National policy will be laid in the pure and immutable principles of private morality; and the pre-eminence of a free Government, be exemplified by all the attributes which can win the affections of its Citizens, and command the respect of the world.

© **Barbara M. Peller**

I dwell on this prospect with every satisfaction which an ardent love for my Country can inspire: since there is no truth more thoroughly established, than that there exists in the economy and course of nature, an indissoluble union between virtue and happiness, between duty and advantage, between the genuine maxims of an honest and magnanimous policy, and the solid rewards of public prosperity and felicity: Since we ought to be no less persuaded that the propitious smiles of Heaven, can never be expected on a nation that disregards the eternal rules of order and right, which Heaven itself has ordained: And since the preservation of the sacred fire of liberty, and the destiny of the Republican model of Government, are justly considered as deeply, perhaps as finally staked, on the experiment entrusted to the hands of the American people.

Besides the ordinary objects submitted to your care, it will remain with your judgment to decide, how far an exercise of the occasional power delegated by the Fifth article of the Constitution is rendered expedient at the present juncture by the nature of objections which have been urged against the System, or by the degree of inquietude which has given birth to them. Instead of undertaking particular recommendations on this subject, in which I could be guided by no lights derived from official opportunities, I shall again give way to my entire confidence in your discernment and pursuit of the public good: For I assure myself that whilst you carefully avoid every alteration which might endanger the benefits of an United and effective Government, or which ought to await the future lessons of experience; a reverence for the characteristic rights of freemen, and a regard for the public harmony, will sufficiently influence your deliberations on the question how far the former can be more impregnably fortified, or the latter be safely and advantageously promoted.

To the preceeding observations I have one to add, which will be most properly addressed to the House of Representatives. It concerns myself, and will therefore be as brief as possible. When I was first honoured with a call into the Service of my Country, then on the eve of an arduous struggle for its liberties, the light in which I contemplated my duty required that I should renounce every pecuniary compensation. From this resolution I have in no instance departed. And being still under the impressions which produced it, I must decline as inapplicable to myself, any share in the personal emoluments, which may be indispensably included in a permanent provision for the Executive Department; and must accordingly pray that the pecuniary estimates for the Station in which I am placed, may, during my continuance in it, be limited to such actual expenditures as the public good may be thought to require.

Having thus imported to you my sentiments, as they have been awakened by the occasion which brings us together, I shall take my present leave; but not without resorting once more to the benign parent of the human race, in humble supplication that since he has been pleased to favour the American people, with opportunities for deliberating in perfect tranquility, and dispositions for deciding with unparellelled unanimity on a form of Government, for the security of their Union, and the advancement of their happiness; so his divine blessing may be equally conspicuous in the enlarged views, the temperate consultations, and the wise measures on which the success of this Government must depend.

Answer Section
(with some additional background information)

ANSWERS AND ADDITIONAL BACKGROUND INFORMATION

Benjamin Franklin: "Join or Die"
1. It was possible for these newspapers and other entities to use the material without permission because there were no copyright laws at that time.
2. The abbreviations are as follows: N.E. = New England, N.Y. = New York, N.J. = New Jersey, P = Pennsylvania, M = Maryland, V = Virginia, N.C. = North Carolina, and S.C. = South Carolina.
It is surprising because Delaware and Georgia are not included and Connecticut, New Hampshire, Vermont, and Massachusetts are all combined into New England.
Delaware was probably omitted because it shared a governor with Pennsylvania even though it had its own legislature. Starting at the head, the colonies are shown from north to south, almost like a map.
3. During this period of time there was a widespread superstition that if the pieces of a snake were put together, the snake could come back to life. The parts of the snake represented the individual states, which would have no power. Together, the colonies could have power, just like the revitalized snake.
4. Answers will vary, but it elicits fear, a common propaganda tool. This cartoon accomplishes it in a subtle, intellectual way.
5. Most will probably say that it is a valid point. An either/or fallacy assumes that there are only 2 possible positions in an argument or approaches to a situation. In reality, there are usually more than 2 options.

The Stamp Act
1. The French and Indian Wars, known in Britain as the Seven Years' War, took place from 1756 to 1763. Britain was in need of revenue to pay for that costly war. It sought to raise money to pay for that as well as the cost of stationing troops in the colonies by regulating colonial trade. This and other acts reflect this practice.
2. The request is aimed at King George III.
3. The Declaratory Act reaffirmed Parliament's right to legislate and, therefore, tax the colonists. Many of the colonists believed that they had the right to legislate themselves.

The Stamp Act: Protests
1. The missing words are "tarring" and "feathering."
2. The words "Liberty Tree" are on the tree. That is where the Boston branch of the Sons of Liberty met. The artist was against the group. The visual shows the violent nature of their protests. They seem to be laughing and enjoying their cruelty.
3. The newspapers called the stamp "fatal." The use of the skull and crossbones as "an emblem of the effects of the stamp" infers that the stamps will be the death of newspapers.
4. A broadside is a one-sheet handout. The notice asks protesters to meet in order to ensure the resignation of Andrew Oliver.
Background:
Although Andrew Oliver was not a proponent of the Stamp Act, he was about to be put in charge of enforcing it. A crowd of angry protesters, led by the Sons of Liberty, went to his home and caused a lot of damage, both inside and out. Oliver was forced to publicly resign his post.
5. They will meet under Liberty on December 17, 1765, at noon.
6. The Sons of Liberty chose this place because everyone knew it meant that they were to meet under the Liberty Tree.
7. People were usurping the name Sons of Liberty and using it to serve their own purposes. The creator of the notice wanted to be sure people knew that the true members of the Sons of Liberty were making the request.
8. The lower-case "s" is f-like in appearance. The word "the" is repeated.

The Stamp Act: Repeal
1. Unjust acts (all Imposts without Parliament) are about to be buried. The funeral procession is portrayed. The creator shows his bias against the Stamp Act.
2. Anti-Sejanus will lead the procession. The burial service and the sermon are in his hands. The sermon is signed Anti-Sejanus. He is actually the Reverend W. Scott, who supported the Stamp Act using that pseudonym.
3. It served to further mock and humiliate the supporters of the Stamp Act.

4. George Stamp represents George Grenville. The Stamp Act—"Miss Americ Stamp, who was born in 1763 and died hard in 1766"—is in the coffin.
5. The numbers 71 and 122 refer to the number of votes against the repeal of the Stamp Act in the House of Lords and House of Commons.
6. They represent the Parliamentary leaders responsible for the repeal of the bill. The Marques of Rockingham, who had recently been named Prime Minister, convinced Parliament of the benefits of this repeal. The ships are part of what is described as a "joyful scene." The ships are now ready to carry the goods to America.
7. The dog's action adds humiliation to the supporters of the act.
8. The purpose of the broadside was to mock those in Parliament who had supported the Stamp Act.

The Boston Massacre
1. Answers will vary, but Adams knew that it would not be popular among the colonists. He would not want to have alienated groups like the Sons of Liberty. His family might have been endangered if people protested his decision violently. He risked losing business for his law practice. On the positive side, he might have believed in the principle that everyone deserves a fair trial. Some historians have suggested that he might have been promised the legislative seat that he won after the trial.
2. The actual scene was chaotic. The soldiers would not have been lined up to fire. It should have been nighttime. There should be snow. (Some colonists had thrown snowballs.) The print shows seven soldiers plus Captain Preston, but there were really eight. Also, there was no ice or snow in the scene.
3. The name of the Customs House was changed to Butchers Hall.
4. It supports his guilt by portraying him with his sword in the air as if giving the order to fire. However, Captain Preston was acquitted.
5. Answers will vary.

The Boston Tea Party: Broadside
1. The notice was published in Philadelphia. The meeting day is the same day that a smaller version of the tea party was held there.
2. The purpose was to tell everyone where and when to meet to discuss what to do about the British tea ship that had arrived.
3. The notice said that it was important in order to preserve the liberty of America.

The Boston Tea Party: Engraving
1. Answers will vary, but it is very possible because the men who left the meeting went to carry out the plan to dump the tea.
2. Answers will vary, but they might have wanted to serve as a distraction while the men went to the harbor to dump the tea.
3. The British saw the acts as a means of getting the colonists to obey the laws they had imposed upon them. The colonists saw them as being intolerable because they were passed without them having any representation. They especially disliked the idea of troops being sent to enforce the laws.
4. Some of the colonists on board the ships dressed like Mohawk Indians.
5. The men are dumping the tea into the water.
6. An axe is seen. They would have needed something to break open the chests of tea.
7. The illustration shows people standing along the shore watching. (This may be difficult to see.)

Patrick Henry: "Give Me Liberty or Give Me Death!"
1. Henry was extremely polite. He praised their patriotism and their abilities. He asked them not to think him disrespectful. In no way does he attack them for their views. Answers to the second part will vary.
2. It gave the delegates the idea of that Henry's views would differ from theirs. According to Henry, he wanted to arrive at the truth.
3. Answers might vary, but some of what he said might have been considered treasonous. It might have been dangerous for him to put it in writing.
4. The meaning of "awful" during that period of time stressed the root "awe." Henry was stressing the importance of their discussion and the fact that their decision would have life-changing consequences.

© **Barbara M. Peller**

5. Henry alluded to the Sirens, whose song was irresistable. He said, "Listen to the song of the siren till she transforms us into beasts." He compared "the illusion of hope" to the call of the siren. It is tempting to listen to it but it can be dangerous. The hope he referred to was the hope of negotiating an acceptable peace.
6. He was addressing Peyton Randolph, president of the Virginia Convention.
7. He used these verbs to reinforce the fact that they had tried to maintain peace: *petitioned, remonstrated, supplicated, prostrated,* and *implored*.
8. "We have prostrated ourselves before King George III."
9. "Give me liberty or give me death" is an example of an either-or fallacy. This type of logical fallacy is often used in propaganda. In this case, Henry intentionally presented only two possible options: liberty or death. He uses this tactic to convince his fellow delegates that there is no choice but to fight. Choosing not to fight would mean slavery, which would be unacceptable.
10. The setting is the Virginia Assembly. The papers on the floor say, "Proceedings of the Virginia Assembly."
11. Many of the delegates at the meeting were loyal to Britain and went to the meeting in favor of taking conciliatory measures. Henry's persuasive speech convinced them to vote in support of his resolutions.

Common Sense: Cover

1. The pamphlet was published by R. Bell in Philadelphia.
2. The target audience were the Inhabitants of America.
3. It was published in 1776.
4. These are the 4 subjects:
   I. Of the Origin and Design of Government in General, with Concise Remarks on the English Constitution
   II. Of Monarchy and Hereditary Succession
   III. Thoughts on the Present State of American Affairs
   IV. Of the Present Ability of America: with some Miscellaneous Reflections

The subjects start out general, talking about government, the monarchy, and hereditary succession. The last two deal with conditions in America.

5. It probably belonged to Hamilton's son William.

Common Sense: Excerpts

1. Paine saw government as a necessary evil: "Government, even in its best state, is but a necessary evil; in its worst state an intolerable one." Its main purpose is to provide security; therefore, it should be judged by how effective it is at providing that security. "Wherefore, security being the true design and end of government, it unanswerably follows that whatever form thereof appears most likely to ensure it to us, with the least expense and greatest benefit, is preferable to all others."
2. Paine believed that society is created as a result of our wants and government as a result of our vices: "Society is produced by our wants, and government by our wickedness; the former promotes our happiness POSITIVELY by uniting our affections, the latter NEGATIVELY by restraining our vices."
3. He believed that there was no natural or religious reason why kings should be distinguished from their subjects. "But there is another and great distinction for which no truly natural or religious reason can be assigned, and that is the distinction of men into KINGS and SUBJECTS."
4. He believed that the idea of hereditary succession was absurd. He said that would be okay if it produced good and wise leaders, but it does not. "But it is not so much the absurdity as the evil of hereditary succession which concerns mankind. Did it ensure a race of good and wise men it would have the seal of divine authority, but as it opens a door to the FOOLISH, the WICKED, and the IMPROPER, it hath in it the nature of oppression. Men who look upon themselves born to reign, and others to obey, soon grow insolent."
5. He said there was no advantage to remaining with Britain: "I challenge the warmest advocate for reconciliation to show a single advantage that this continent can reap by being connected with Great Britain." Also, he believed Europe would trade with them directly: "I repeat the challenge; not a single advantage is derived. Our corn will fetch its price in any market in Europe, and our imported goods must be paid for buy them where we will."
Disadvantages included the fact that they were brought into European conflicts; it set them against nations they would otherwise find friendly; and it interfered with trade with Europe. "But the injuries and disadvantages which we sustain by that connection, are without number…dependence on, Great Britain, tends directly to involve this Continent in European wars and quarrels, and set us at variance with nations who would otherwise seek our friendship, and against whom we have neither anger nor complaint. As Europe is our market for trade, we ought to form no partial connection with any part of it."
6. He said that their strength is in uniting: "'Tis not in numbers but in unity that our great strength lies." He also said that when the colonies got larger and developed self-interests, it might be harder to join together.

Declaration of Independence: John Trumbull Painting
1. They are the five men on the committee to draft the document. (Left to right they are John Adams, Roger Sherman, Robert Livingston, Thomas Jefferson, and Benjamin Franklin.) Thomas Jefferson is the one handing over the document.
2. John Hancock, president of the Continental Congress, is the one receiving the document.

Declaration of Independence: Excerpts from the Document
1. The introduction states that the purpose of the document is to state the causes that led to the need to separate from the British Empire.
2. The inevitable truths are as follows:
    - all men are created equal;
    - all men have basic human rights—life, liberty, and the pursuit of happiness; and
    - those rights are given to them by God.
3. Government's role is to protect those rights, and government must be by the consent of the governed.
4. The function of the body was to name the colonies' grievances against King George III.
5. The Declaration of Independence did not actually form the United States of America; it called for the individual colonies to act as nations with the right to levy war and make alliances with other countries.
6. They pledged to fight to protect one another.

Marquis de Lafayette
1. According to the print, they met in Philadelphia on August 3, 1777.
2. The mood seems formal but cordial. The two principal men seem glad to be meeting.
3. The people appear to be wealthy. They seem aristocratic.
4. It tells us that they had developed a close friendship. One clue is that he addressed him as "my dear Marq." Another is that Washington refers to "endearing expressions of attachment" and says that these expressions are "a counterpart of my own feelings for you." He says that his letters are welcome. Also, their wives exchanged their "best compliments."

Surrender of General Burgoyne at Saratoga: Key to Trumbull's Painting
Left to Right:
1. Major Lithcow, Massachusetts
2. Colonel Cilly, New Hampshire
3. General Stark, New Hampshire
4. Captain Seymour, of Shelton's House
5. Major Hull, Massachusetts
6. Colonel Greaton, Massachusetts
7. Major Dearborne, New Hampshire
8. Colonell Scammell, New Hampshire
9. Colonel Lewis, Quartermaster General, New Hampshire
10. Major General Phillips, British
11. Lieuenant General Burgoyne, British SURRENDERING HIS SWORD TO GENERAL GATES
12. General Baron Riedesel, Germany
13. Colonel Wilkinson, Deputy Adjutant General, American
14. General Gates RECEIVING THE SWORD FROM GENERAL BURGOYNE
15. Colonel Prescott, Massachusetts, Volunteers
16. Colonel Morgan, Virginia Rifleman
17. Brigadier General Rufus Putnam, Massachusetts
18. Lieutenant Colonel John Brooks, late Governor of Massachusetts
19. Rev. Mr. Hitchcock, chaplain, Rhode Island
20. Major Rob Troup, Aide-de-camp, New York
21. Major Haskell
22. Major Armstrong
23. Major General Philip Schuyler, Albany
24. Brigadier General Glover, Massachusetts
25. Brigadier General Whipple, New Hampshire Militia
26. Major M. Clarkson, Aide-de-camp, New York

Surrender of General Burgoyne at Saratoga: Key to Trumbull's Painting
1. He is the one to the left of the man in the center with both arms outstretched. He is offering his sword.
2. He is in the center of the painting with both arms outstretched. Burgoyne is offering him his sword.
3. Gates is showing Burgoyne respect by not accepting the sword.
4. Answers may vary, but Trumbull meant him to be pointing to the tent, which held refreshments.
5. He is Reverend Hitchcock, chaplain of Rhode Island.
6. It is a very peaceful scene. Images such as a gently flowing flag and the presence of the chaplain evoke feelings of peace, not war. Also, if seen in color, the blue sky would add to the peaceful image.

Benedict Arnold
1. This is Benedict Arnold's oath of allegiance to the United States, which he signed In 1778. This oath was required of all military officers.
2. His rank was Major General.
3. He signed it May 20, 1778.
4. In 1780 he betrayed this oath of allegiance by conspiring to surrender West Point to the British.
5. The officers had the option of writing "swear" or "affirm." Quakers and some other sects refused to "swear."
6. Henry Knox became the first Secretary of War of the new United States of America.

Spying Techniques
1. They were used to ensure that the contents of a letter could not be understood if correspondence was captured.
2. The recipient placed the paper over the flame of a candle or treated it with a chemical reagent, such as sodium carbonate, which would reveal the letter's hidden contents.
3. These letters enabled him to acquire information about troop movements, supplies, and battle plans that would not otherwise be available to him.
4. The letter and the "mask" were usually delivered by separate couriers to ensure that the trick would go undetected.

Valley Forge
1. Nathanael Greene wrote it. He was Quartermaster General at Valley Forge.
2. It was sent to Joseph Webb, a merchant. He was located in Wethersfield, Connecticut.
3. It was sent on April 2, 1778.
4. Greene was requesting supplies. He asked for medium sized portmanteaus, which are hinged suitcases; valises; and canvas for tents, knapsacks, and mattresses.
5. The franking privilege allowed certain public offices to send official government correspondence for free. (Franking is the act of putting an official mark or signature on a letter or parcel to indicate that postage has been paid or does not need to be paid.)
6. They will be sent to Fishkill, which is in New York.

John Paul Jones
1. It is the French Cross of the Institution of Military Merit, which was presented to him by Louis XVI in 1780. Congress confirmed his acceptance of the French decoration in 1781.
2. The *Serapis* is the one on the right. The lieutenant describes the Serapis as a 44-gun ship; the *Bonhomme Richard* was barely sea worthy. He also wrote, "There was not a man on board the *Bon Homme Richard* ignorant of the superiority of the *Serapis*."
3. A broadside is a nearly simultaneous firing of all the guns from one side of a warship. The order was given on both warships at about the same time.
4. In an attempt to separate the ships, the *Serapis* let go her anchor.
5. In Naval terminology to "strike the colors" means to haul down the ship's flag to signify surrender.
6. It surrendered between 10 and 11 o'clock.
7. The first lieutenant of the *Serapis* thought the *Bonhomme Richard* had surrendered and asked Captain Pearson whether the ship alongside had struck to him. The fact that the *Serapis* surrendered was a surprise because both the ship was superior and the crew was more experienced.

Paying for the War: Robert Morris
1. "Specie" refers to coins and other forms of metal used as money.
2. America is represented by the man with feathered cap cutting the horns off a cow. The cow represents British commerce, which is being milked by a Dutchman. The two men holding bowls of milk represent France and Spain, who have given aid to the Americans.
3. The lion, which represents the stronger Britain, is asleep. The small dog, which is normally less powerful, represents America; it is standing on the lion's back urinating. A distraught Englishman is standing to the left of the lion.
Additional Information: In the background, across an expanse of water, is a city labeled "Philadelphia;" to the left of the city is a ship, the "Eagle," laid-up in dry dock; Admiral Howe is sitting at a table, out of sight of his flag ship, with his brother General Howe. A keg is on the ground to the left, and wine bottles are on the ground to the right of the table.
4. Its purpose was to commemorate Morris's financial services during the Revolutionary War.
5. Mercury is handing a bag of gold to Robert Morris. We know it is Mercury because of the winged cap and sandals and caduceus.
6. To the left, men move a box on a dolly; on the right, the anchor and sailors lead into "Marine."
7. The next scene is "Marine." The anchor and sailors lead viewers into that scene.
Additional Background: "The Apotheosis of Washington" is the fresco painted by Greek-Italian artist Constantino Brumidi in 1865 and visible through the oculus of the dome in the rotunda of the United States Capitol Building. The fresco is suspended 180 feet (55 m) above the rotunda floor and covers an area of 4,664 square feet (433.3 m2). The figures painted are up to 15 feet (4.6 m) tall and are visible from the floor below. The dome was completed in 1863, and Brumidi painted it over the course of 11 months at the end of the Civil War. He was paid $40,000 ($625,826 in today's funds[1]) for the fresco.
8. "Apotheosis" means "the highest point in the development of something; the elevation of someone to divine status." Answers will vary as to the evaluation of the title.

Paying for the War: Haym Salomon
1. The cause was the fight for independence. Salomon contributed by doing a lot to finance the war.
2. Four colonists were recognized in the Contributors to the Cause set of four stamps. The four included Sybil Ludington, Salem Poor, Haym Salomon, and Francisco.
The first stamp commemorated Sybil Ludington. She was born and raised in Putnam County, New York. Her father, Colonel Henry Ludington, commanded a military regiment there. In the face of danger at the age of 16, she rode 40 miles through New York and Connecticut to rally the militia to the cry, "The British are burning Danbury. Muster at Ludington's." Although Danbury was burned, Sybil's ride resulted in a militia victory which cost the British a tenth of their attacking force and put them in retreat.
The second stamp in the Contributors to the Cause Series was Salem Poor. Poor was a celebrated African-American soldier who fought at the Battle of Bunker Hill. Fourteen officers signed a commendation citing him for bravery.
The third stamp commemorated Haym Salomon. Born in Poland, this Jewish merchant and banker raised much of the money that financed the Revolution. Twice imprisoned by the British, he continued to donate freely to the American cause, only to die penniless after the war.
Last in the Contributors to the Cause Series, Francisco is remembered for his incredible bravery and strength. He is said to have brandished a five-foot broadsword. He is shown carrying a heavy cannon, weighing 1,000 pounds, at the Battle of Camden, where he saved the life of his commander.
3. Answers will vary, but he sacrificed his own well being to advance the cause.

Siege of Yorktown: Articles of Capitulation
1. Article III stated that "the garrison of York will march out to a place to be appointed in front of the posts, at two o'clock precisely, with shouldered arms, colors cased, and drums beating a British or German march. They are then to ground their arms, and return to their encampments, where they will remain until they are dispatched to the places of their destination."
2. By allowing Cornwallis unregulated use of the sloop *Bonetta* for carrying dispatches to British headquarters in New York City, Washington was allowing Cornwallis to facilitate the escape of Loyalists and American deserters. Many wanted to see them punished.
3. It dealt with how the sick and wounded would be treated.

Siege of Yorktown: Lithograph
1. No, it did not give an accurate account of the event. Cornwallis was not actually present at the formal surrender. He had sent his second in command. Answers will vary as to whether or not it still gave a good idea of the event.
2. The Americans are all smiling. The British are grim.
3. Answers will vary.
4. These things reinforce the idea that they were surrounded.

Articles of Confederation
1. The Radicals had more influence. Article II states that "each state retains its sovereignty, freedom, and independence, and every power, jurisdiction, and right, which is not by this confederation expressly delegated to the United States, in Congress assembled."
2. Under the Articles of Confederation, no provision was made for an executive branch to enforce the laws nor for a national court system—a judicial branch—to interpret them. The Confederation Congress, a legislative branch of government, was the sole organ of the national government, but it had no power to force the states to do anything against their will.

Treaty of Paris: Document
1. Independence from Great Britain was addressed in Article 1st.: "His Brittanic Majesty acknowledges the said United States, viz., New Hampshire, Massachusetts Bay, Rhode Island and Providence Plantations, Connecticut, New York, New Jersey, Pennsylvania, Delaware, Maryland, Virginia, North Carolina, South Carolina and Georgia, to be free sovereign and Independent States; that he treats with them as such, and for himself his Heirs & Successors, relinquishes all claims to the Government, Propriety, and Territorial Rights of the same and every Part thereof."

Borders were dealt with in Article 2d: "And that all Disputes which might arise in future on the subject of the Boundaries of the said United States may be prevented, it is hereby agreed and declared, that the following are and shall be their Boundaries:..." The article goes on to specify the details.

Fishing rights were dealt with in Article 3rd: "It is agreed that the People of the United States shall continue to enjoy unmolested the Right to take Fish of every kind on the Grand Bank and on all the other Banks of Newfoundland..." It goes on to name several places and some restrictions.

Treatment of Loyalists is addressed in Article 6th: "That there shall be no future Confiscations made nor any Prosecutions commenced against any Person or Persons for, or by Reason of the Part, which he or they may have taken in the present War, and that no Person shall on that Account suffer any future Loss or Damage, either in his Person, Liberty, or Property; and that those who may be in Confinement on such Charges at the Time of the Ratification of the Treaty in America shall be immediately set at Liberty, and the Prosecutions so commenced be discontinued."

2. It was signed in Paris on September 3, 1783.
3. **For the Americans:**

John Adams was born in Massachusetts. He was a critic of Great Britain's authority in colonial America and viewed the British imposition of high taxes and tariffs as a tool of oppression. Adams served as a delegate to the Continental Congress. He would later become the second President of the United States.

Benjamin Franklin was born in Boston. He established a successful printing business in Philadelphia. He helped launch a lending library, hospital and college in Philadelphia. He also experimented with electricity, among other scientific projects. Franklin served in the Second Continental Congress and helped draft the Declaration of Independence in 1776.

John Jay was born in New York and drafted the state's first constitution in 1777. In 1778 he was chosen president of the Continental Congress. He then became U.S. minister to Spain. John Jay later served as the first chief justice of the U.S. Supreme Court.

For the British:

David Hartley, the Younger, was born in Bath, Somerset, England. He was a radical English pamphleteer, a member of the House of Commons and an inventor. He became a close friend of Benjamin Franklin, whom he had met in London. He had believed that a peaceful reconciliation between Great Britain and the North American colonies was possible; he had spoken and written against the conflict.

4. The marks are the men's official seals.

Treaty of Paris of 1783: the Painting
1. This was meant to include the British commissioners as well, but they refused to pose, and the picture was never finished.
2. Answers will vary.

Shay's Rebellion: Cover of Bickerstaff's *Boston Almanack* of 1787
1. They are intentionally drawn in an unattractive manner. It seems unlikely that the artist empathized with these men.
2. Both Shays and Shattuck are holding swords and are wearing the uniform of a soldier in the Continental Army. This symbolizes their roles as leaders in the movement. Shadduck is holding a flag, implying that the danger may be to the government. The cannon in the background shows that the military threat is serious.

Shay's Rebellion: Washington's and Jefferson's Letters
Washington's Letters
1. Letter to Henry Lee: Americans were doing a poor job of governing themselves and he was embarrassed by that fact.
2. Letter to David Humphreys: He said that England was right in believing that the colonists would struggle when trying to govern themselves.
3. Letter to Henry Knox: Washington believed that a weak government would lead to continued chaos.

Jefferson's Letters:
1. Letter to William S. Smith: Jefferson thought that the rebellion was a positive event because it revitalized the concept of self-government.
2. First Letter to James Madison: He was saying that a little rebellion was necessary in a strong government.
3. Second Letter to James Madison: He believed that even a strong central government cannot completely prevent opposition.
4. Letter to Abigail Adams: He believed that being allowed to rebel was important, even when the cause is not worthy of the rebellion.

Comparison
George Washington believed that the government was not doing a good job at self-governing. He was extremely embarrassed by the fact that other nations, especially England, would realize this and that England would feel as though it was correct in its belief that the American would not be successful at governing itself.
Thomas Jefferson believed that Shays' Rebellion—in fact any rebellion—was a good thing because it helped to ensure the people's liberty and to limit the power of the government. He also believed that no government—no matter how strong—could completely prevent opposition from time to time.

The United States Constitution
1. New Hampshire was the ninth state to ratify the Constitution.
2. James Madison took copious notes during the Constitutional Convention. Delegates referred to his notes throughout the discussions and debates.
3. Like many other Anti-Federalists, they believed the document should include a bill of rights to protect the rights of the individual.
4. Answers will vary.

The Federalist
1. All three men had been delegates to the Constitutional Convention. They had all been responsible in part for the creation of the document. Answers will vary, but maybe they wanted the essays to appear to be more objective and less biased in their point of view.
2. Publius Valerius Publicola is credited with having an important role in the founding of the Roman Empire. Answers will vary as to why they chose him. Perhaps they felt they would be instrumental in the founding of this new nation.
3. Since New York and Virginia did not ratify the document until after it became the law of the land, *The Federalist* most likely did not contribute greatly to its ratification. It did, however, add greatly to our understanding of the document.
4. Most wanted a bill of rights such as the one later added.

5. The note at the bottom suggests that the copy originally belonged to Jefferson. We can infer from the note at the top that it was a gift from Elizabeth (Schuyler) Hamilton, wife of Alexander Hamilton, to her sister, Angelica Schuler Church.

The Federalist: Advertisement
1. The purpose of the ad was to encourage people to push for ratification of the Constitution.
2. According to the ad, the Federalist is a collection of essays written by a citizen of New York in favor of the constitution.
3. It will be in the form of one handsome Volume duodecimo, which results from the folding of each printed sheet into 12 leaves.
4. Most of the copies will be printed on fine paper, but a few will be printed on superfine royal writing paper. Those on the superfine paper will cost more.
5. William Duer wrote in support of the Federalist authors under the name "Philo-Publius," or "Friend of Publius." The pseudonym "Publius" was used by the 3 Federalist authors.

Washington's First Inauguration
1. A vicissitude is a change of circumstances or fortune, usually one that is thought to be unwelcome or unpleasant. Answers will vary to the second part.
2. He was honored to have been summoned by the country and entrusted with such an important responsibility, but he had been planning on retiring and regaining his health.
3. He hoped he was up to the task. He had no experience in civil administration. He hoped that his past successes and the praise of his fellow citizens hadn't led him to believe he was more qualified than he really was. He hoped that if he had overestimated his belief in his qualifications, people would realize he had good intentions.
4. Article Five of the United States Constitution describes the process whereby the Constitution may be altered. Washington wanted Congress to consider a bill of rights.
5. He did not want to receive payment for his service as President. He only wanted to be repaid for expenses. However, Article II, Section 1 of the United States Constitution requires that the president receives payment. "The President shall, at stated times, receive for his services, a compensation, which shall neither be increased nor diminished during the period for which he shall have been elected, and he shall not receive within that period any other emolument from the United States, or any of them." He received $25,000.

The Bill of Rights
1. The Amendment provides that "No law, varying the compensation for the services of the Senators and Representatives, shall take effect, until an election of representatives shall have intervened."
2. The First Amendment ensures freedom of religion, speech, the press, peaceable assembly, and petition.

The Second Amendment ensures the right to keep and bear arms.

The Third Amendment ensures that troops will not be quartered in citizens' homes without permission.

The Fourth Amendment ensures protection against unreasonable search and seizure.

The Fifth Amendment ensures protection against the taking of life, liberty, or property without due process of law; it ensures protection against self-incrimination.

The Sixth Amendment ensures that a person accused of a crime has a right to a defense lawyer, to a speedy and public trial, to hear charges, to call witnesses, and to be present when witnesses speak in court.

The Seventh Amendment ensures that in federal civil trials the accused has the right to trial by jury.

The Eighth Amendment ensures protection against excessive bail and cruel and unusual punishment.

The Ninth Amendment ensures that the rights enumerated in the Constitution are not a person's only rights.

The Tenth Amendment ensures that powers not delegated to the federal government nor prohibited to the states are reserved to the states or to the people.

Document Analysis Sheets

Cartoon Analysis Worksheet

Level 1

Visuals	Words (not all cartoons include words)
1. List the objects or people you see in the cartoon.	1. Identify the cartoon caption and/or title.
	2. Locate three words or phrases used by the cartoonist to identify objects or people within the cartoon.
	3. Record any important dates or numbers that appear in the cartoon.

Level 2

Visuals	Words
2. Which of the objects on your list are symbols?	4. Which words or phrases in the cartoon appear to be the most significant? Why do you think so?
3. What do you think each symbol means?	5. List adjectives that describe the emotions portrayed in the cartoon.

Level 3

A. Describe the action taking place in the cartoon.

Limit response for each question to 3 lines of text

B. Explain how the words in the cartoon clarify the symbols.

C. Explain the message of the cartoon.

D. What special interest groups would agree/disagree with the cartoon's message? Why?

**Designed and developed by the
Education Staff, National Archives and Records Administration,
Washington, DC 20408**

Photo Analysis Worksheet

Step 1. Observation

A. Study the photograph for 2 minutes. Form an overall impression of the photograph and then examine individual items. Next, divide the photo into quadrantes an study each section to see what new details become visible.

B. Use the chart below to list people, objects, and activities in the photograph.

People	Objects	Activities

Step 2. Inference

Limit response for each question to 5 lines of text

Based on what you have observed above, list three things you might infer from this photograph.

Step 3. Questions

A. What questions does this photograph raise in your mind?

B. Where could you find answers to them?

**Designed and developed by the
Education Staff, National Archives and Records Administration,
Washington, DC 20408**

© Barbara M. Peller   *Using Primary Sources to Teach U.S. History: The American Revolution*

Written Document Analysis Worksheet

1. **TYPE OF DOCUMENT (Check one):**
   - ○ Newspaper
   - ○ Letter
   - ○ Patent
   - ○ Memorandum
   - ○ Map
   - ○ Telegram
   - ○ Press Release
   - ○ Report
   - ○ Advertisement
   - ○ Congressional Record
   - ○ Census Report
   - ○ Other

2. **UNIQUE PHYSICAL CHARACTERISTICS OF THE DOCUMENT (Check one or more):**
   - ☐ Interesting Letterhead
   - ☐ Handwritten
   - ☐ Typed
   - ☐ Seals
   - ☐ Notations
   - ☐ "RECEIVED" stamp
   - ☐ Other

3. **DATE(S) OF DOCUMENT:**

4. **AUTHOR (OR CREATOR) OF THE DOCUMENT:**

   POSITION (TITLE):

5. **FOR WHAT AUDIENCE WAS THE DOCUMENT WRITTEN?**

6. **DOCUMENT INFORMATION** (There are many possible ways to answer A-E.) Limit response for each question to 3 lines of text

   A. List three things the author said that you think are important:

   B. Why do you think this document was written?

   C. What evidence in the document helps you know why it was written? Quote from the document.

   D. List two things the document tells you about life in the United States at the time it was written.

   E. Write a question to the author that is left unanswered by the document:

Designed and developed by the Education Staff, National Archives and Records Administration, Washington, DC 20408